Family Business Matters

How to make your family business a success

Harry Moore

About the author

 Dr Harry Moore MBE has had a lifelong career in the corporate world and the professions and is a recognised and well established specialist in business turnaround with a particular emphasis on SMEs and family businesses.

He was a senior manager at Dunlop Ltd, Chairman and Managing Director of Silver Cross Prams Ltd, Managing Director of HunterPrint plc and Collets International. Harry was also a Principal at KPMG, enjoying partner status and held a similar position at Coopers & Lybrand, now PwC. At both firms he led business turnaround teams. He has also worked with the UK Government's Small Business Service as an Advisor Manager where he designed and managed a business recovery scheme that saved 135 businesses. He also delivered an advisory service to family businesses on behalf of the UK Government and was an appointed family business advisor to Coutts Bank of London. He founded his own turnaround and family business practice – Moore

Fleming. This has now been acquired by NMS Consulting Inc where Harry is Senior Partner – Head of Europe and Head of the Global Transformation Team.

He is a Doctor of the University of Loughborough and was awarded an MBE by HM the Queen of England for his services to charities. He and his wife set up the COPE Children's Cancer Unit, The Laura Centre – a bereavement service for those affected by the death of a child and Rainbows Children's Hospice.

This guide is based on his experiences in the above professional firms coupled with his hands on experience in the real world of running businesses.

Books by Harry Moore

Non-fiction – Business

Business Turnaround – How to do it

Family Business Matters

Autobiographical Novel

A Lark Ascending

Fiction

Aldora

How can you sing that love is sweet?

Fat Cats on Thin Ice

The Green Monk and other tales

I was a flower

Pathétique

Poems

I wonder if you wonder

Copyright Harry Moore 2021

Harry Moore has asserted his right under the UK Copyright, Design and Patents Act 1988 to be identified as the author of this work.

ISBN: 9798503649352

Published by

Longhirst Publishing

Park Place,

St James's Street

London SW1A 1LR

Contents

1. *Introduction*
2. *Background*
3. *Family business dynamics*
4. *Planning for success*
5. *Setting the business objectives*
6. *The Strategic Workshop*
    - 6.1. Personal objectives
    - 6.2. Corporate objectives
    - 6.3. Reconciliation of objectives
7. *Developing our strategy*
    - 7.1. Achieving the strategic objectives
    - 7.2. Building the future business model
8. *The family business plan*
    - 8.1. Organic growth.
    - 8.2. Growth through diversification.
    - 8.3. Strategic Growth
9. *Culture*
10. *Shareholding*

11. *Communication*
    - 11.1. Sunday Lunch Syndrome.
    - 11.2. The family v business differential.
    - 11.3. Engaging with staff.

12. *Take good care of my baby*
    - 12.1 Succession Planning
    - 12.2. The Succession Plan
    - 12.2. Choosing the right successor
    - 12.3. Developing the family successor
    - 12.4. Grooming
    - 12.5. The personality of the successor
    - 12.6. Appropriate further education
    - 12.7. Post education development
    - 12.8. Integrating into the business.
    - 12.9. Letting go

13. *Leadership*
    - 13.1. What makes successful leaders?
    - 13.2. Consultation
    - 13.3. Empowerment

- 13.4. Creativity
- 13.5 Leading through uncertain times
- 13.6. Mentoring in the leadership role

14. Exiting the family business.
- 14.1. Management Buy Out
- 14.2. Selling to a third party.

1. Introduction

Running a business is not easy and for most people life is more comfortable as an employee rather than employer. At its worst managing a business can be likened to warfare; with the potential enemies being manifold in the form of competition, costs, market forces, adverse economic trends, access to resources etc. As if this isn't enough, if you are running a family business it can be almost like fighting a war on two fronts; there is the business and its issues on the one side and the family and their needs on the other and reconciliation of the two can often be challenging, and, in some cases, totally impossible. It's a matter of having to cope with two agendas. All businesses and organisations must cope with the mixture of personal and corporate needs and, in particular, the desires and objectives of the individuals managing the enterprise. With a family business the added challenge is that the personal side will include people who may not actually be employed in the business but who may be owners, family members dependent on the business for their income or family members who may simply influence the decision-making process through relationships with managers or owners.

Family decisions are often driven by emotion, whereas business decisions are, or should be, driven by strategic need. Families do not like change whereas business needs to change to adapt to market trends and forces. Families are also risk averse whereas business managers often must take considered commercial risks. In fact, business itself is risk taking as no one can be certain of future economic and market trends. However, there are many shared values and many things in common that drive or influence their respective entities. For example, they are both driven by economic need. As a minimum the family must generate regular income to put food on the table and may also be driven by a desire to create wealth to enjoy an enhanced lifestyle or build reserves for future generations. The business also has to maintain an income stream and, if run properly, will want to ensure it has reserves for future financial commitments as well as the working capital to either maintain the business or achieve sustainable growth. These mean that business and family are integrated in terms of their common fiduciary needs and objectives. However, it can be argued that this is no different to that of an owner managed business. In fact, the distinction between the family business and the owner managed business is a thin one in that owner managers can also be influenced by their family members and often are. Accordingly, the contents of this book are, in many ways, relevant to both business models.

So, what is the definition of a family business? Different criteria are used by various specialists or 'experts'. One common definition is that if the business is more than 50% owned by members of the same family and is managed by them then it is a family business. However, there are cases where, for example, there has been significant investment by an outside party, such as a venture capitalist, which means the family owns less than 50%. There are situations where a family owns a business but is no longer directly involved in its management. This could be where the founder has died and there is no successor in the family to manage the business. Accordingly, we cannot be too precise regarding definitions. Overall, if the business is managed by members of one family with significant ownership then it is a family business. The most important element is management rather than ownership as this will determine the culture and values of the business. Having said that, there are businesses owned by families who may have non-executive roles only yet continue to impart their influence upon the running of the business for good or bad. The reality is that if you think you are a family business: you are a family business.

The purpose of this book is to assist family and owner managed businesses to succeed. The definition of success can range from simple survival to empirical growth, depending upon the aims and aspirations of the owners. Some family business only want to achieve a limited level of growth and profitability sufficient to maintain a defined or aspired lifestyle and often with minimal risk. What most family businesses don't want to do is build a business with a view to a potential exit. It is usually not the first thing on their mind at the time of foundation. This generally only happens further down the line if a successor cannot be found from within the family. Families in business tend to be in for the long haul rather than the short haul.

So, this book is about making your family business successful in terms of performance, growth and business continuity and how management and family can ensure success in these areas. It does not address issues of personal finance or tax. There are firms of accountants and financial advisers better equipped to tackle those issues than the author.

Family businesses are the life blood of the economy of all countries. Working with family businesses can be extremely enjoyable and rewarding. It can also be challenging and, at times, frustrating.

2. Background

Several years ago, the UK Government launched an initiative to understand and, perhaps, address the issues that family businesses face. This was following the discovery by the government that the majority of small businesses in the UK were family owned. It was assumed that as family-owned businesses they were managed differently to non-family or corporate organisations and, as a consequence, had to be considered and approached in a different way, almost in has if they were a whole new species. Yes, family businesses are different but, nevertheless, they are still businesses and face the same challenges as non-family enterprises. Following this discovery, which seemed to come almost as a divine revelation, the Government commissioned a survey and the author was asked to manage this. There have been many such surveys since; in the U.K., Europe, the USA and even on a global basis. From the UK survey carried out by my firm Moore Fleming amongst several hundred family businesses across a wide spectrum of business models the two top issues, according to family business owners, were that of succession and communication. No surprise there and repeated surveys by other organisations seem to come up with the same conclusions, ad nauseam.

Following this I carried out a programme of training in the dynamics of family businesses for advisors employed throughout England and Wales by the UK Government sponsored Business Links and for some Chambers of Commerce. This training focused on communication and succession and was intended to help advisors gain a better understanding of the dynamics of working with family businesses.

3. Family business dynamics

Let us be clear on one thing regarding family businesses. They are subject to exactly the same market, economic and commercial forces and trends as any other business whether that be a large corporate or a small sole trader enterprise. Like all businesses the key factor in determining its culture and management style lies in the personalities, wishes and ambitions of its leaders: in this case the family. In addition, every family, like every individual, is different; therefore, we cannot bundle family businesses together and say 'this is what constitutes the basis of a family business'. Yes, there are common dynamics and issues, principally around succession, communication and family participation in the business and its employees. All corporate organisations are influenced by the people that lead them, but also, to some degree, by the people that are led. And even in the family we will get a mixture of personalities and a dominant member or members who will either assume leadership or challenge it, sometimes causing conflict at a board level that permeates throughout the organisation.

Perhaps the biggest frustration amongst staff and, in particular non-family members of the board and senior management is the way that families can frequently change their minds both about the strategic direction of the business and day to day operational matters, and this can happen on a weekly basis. It is what I call the Sunday Lunch Syndrome. This is where agreement has been made on the Friday regarding an issue or a plan of action. Over the weekend the family is together and, inevitably as family business owners do, the business is discussed and, in particular, what was agreed on Friday. Non-executive family members such as the supposedly retiring founders disagree and a different course of action is agreed or the decision is deferred. On Monday management is focused on implementing the actions agreed the previous week only to find that the family has changed its mind and plans something else or nothing at all. This can be a major item or, more often, some detailed day to day matter that non-family managers and staff assume to be their responsibility. This causes frustration and a disinclination on the part of non-family members to make any decisions without referring to a family member.

Working within the family business context for employees, and, indeed, advisers, can sometimes be frustrating, difficult and confusing. Yet, in the majority of family businesses it can be rewarding and enjoyable with a feeling of belonging to the family. This is because the family and the business are all mixed up to such an extent that we may even see employees close to family members involved in child minding, picking up the family owners' children from school and generally sharing in some of the family's personal life, albeit usually from a distance. The family's children working in the business during school holidays or Saturdays is not unusual and staff will tend to welcome them and take special care to look after them. The business is part of the family and in many cases the business can become an extended family community. This feeling of participation brings the employer - the family - and employee closer together and results in harmony, a sharing of values and common goals. Of course, it can have its downside in that some staff may see it as an opportunity to gain favour by being particularly attentive and sycophantic to the needs of these children.

Of course, there are also situations where the family will distance itself from the company's employees to the point of treating family member employees and non-family employees differently. This can be in the form of higher remuneration and benefits to family employees e.g., the daughter who is employed as a sales ledger clerk at an inflated salary and company car. To be successful in terms of staff motivation and good working relationships it is crucial that there is harmonisation between family employees and other staff regarding terms of employment. This is especially important at board level. Otherwise, bitterness and cynicism creep in which can impact upon performance. It is also important for the family members coming into the business to be treated on par with the other employees as they will then have a better understanding of the relation between effort and reward and also integrate with other staff more easily. Many family employers will, in fact, expect more from their children coming into the business than they would expect from non-family employees and make great efforts to ensure that they are not favoured more than others as much as they can. In reality, however, it is unlikely that the family employee will be on a completely equal footing to other employees particularly with regard to securing the top job. Like succession in a royal family, it is expected that the family employee will live up to the task. Sadly, in many cases they fail to do so, much to the detriment of the business and the despair of the founders or parents. The way round this is through sound personal development, training and grooming for the aspired post.

It is said by many family business advisers that families normally do not like change whereas businesses have to adapt to change and thereby lies the perpetual conflict. The family as a unit may not like change but, in my experience, that does not mean that an individual family member, like any other business manager, is not ready to embrace change. The real reason that the family in business is nervous of change is perhaps because the business is their livelihood and a personal as well as financial investment and thereby a risk to their own financial security. They will also be apprehensive that change might affect the stability of the relationship between family and business and their ability to maintain their lifestyle. Accordingly, we often find that a son or daughter new to the business will embark on a programme of change to improve performance but may face some negativity and even open and belligerent resistance from other family members until they are convinced that is not going to be detrimental to their lifestyle and the equilibrium between family and business.

Of course, there are dynamics between family members to consider as well. We can often find that some family members do not get on with each other; some just have different ways of doing things; some are even hostile to each other on occasions; some siblings still have issues with each other that go back to their time in the nursery. We can also have situations where one daughter or son will get on particularly well with their father and the two will agree on most business matters because of that bond. Whereas other siblings will not share that relationship and may even resent father or mother taking too active a role in the business. There is also the situation where one family member will take on more responsibility and be more serious about the business than a brother or sister who may openly abuse their privileged position as a family member by taking too much time off, being late and not taking on sufficient responsibility. They may get away with it because they are favoured by a parent or because the parent does not want to upset the personal relationship they enjoy.

Non-family members of the business need to consider the above of course, but it is more important for family members to recognise how family relations and dynamics can impact upon employees and the running of the business. It means working hard to leave family issues outside the office door as much as possible, or, where they are in relation to the business, to deal with them through a different format such as off-site meetings or through the medium of a family council or board. It also means family members avoiding displaying any personal feelings about relatives to other members of staff and treating family employees as they would any other employee.

4. Planning for success

Success can, of course, come by pure chance; being in the right place at the right time etc. For most of us, however, we have to work towards it. That involves a degree of planning. It does not just happen. It means being ruthlessly focused on achieving our objectives. Businesses that succeed are the ones that plan their future.

In most cases business plans are a waste of time in that they often end up in the bottom of the filing cabinet, only to be brought out when someone wants to explain to a third party the objectives of the company. This is because they are often written to raise finance at the request of lenders or investors. They are also sometimes compiled because external business advisers have recommended it on the basis that they believe every business needs a plan or strategic document. Advisors, who, in the main, have never run a business, often say this as a banket solution for all their clients. The business plan may also have been written because the directors and owners genuinely need to understand where the business is going and to set key milestones to accomplish given objectives. We develop the plan and discuss it with colleagues until we get the final document. We present it to managers and staff and get their full agreement. We then file it somewhere on the server with hard copies in a filing cabinet and then forget about it whilst we get on with the day job.

However, they need not be a waste of time if they are used as a tool to assist in the direction of the business. The written document is less important than what is in the hearts and minds of all employees as to where the business wants to go and how it is to get there. So, the secret to making business plans a success is not to concentrate on the written document. We need to agree on our core objectives, and we need to determine the actions and resources required to achieve these. These need to be instilled into all relevant members of staff, particularly the management team. The business plan should be a living breathing thing whereby everyone knows where they and the organisation are going. There may be elements that we do not wish to share, such as a potential exit strategy, but otherwise it is beneficial to the business if staff have a general indication as to where the company is heading and that they also feel it is their business plan.

A good way to do this is through digital technology. Data and project plans can be kept on a shared drive which is accessible by all employees. Actions can be sent out by email using appropriate CRM based software such as Asana and Pipedrive. The business plan will change as all battle plans have to be adjusted due to prevailing conditions. This does not matter, nor does it mean that the business plan has failed.

So, the message is: forget the written word. This is not important. We must embed all employees with a sense of direction and get their buy in and contribution. By contribution I mean that they will be responsible for their own mini business plan, their own thoughts, and ideas as to how they can help the company achieve its overall strategic objectives. By this empowering of people, you may be amazed at what can be achieved. My own experience is that a little encouragement and empowerment can result in a dramatic improvement in performance. The majority of employees want to be involved.

We should avoid mushroom management whereby staff are kept in the dark and fed with smelly stuff periodically. The analogy, based on a slightly inaccurate assumption about the way mushrooms are cultivated, means that we give employees work without telling them the purpose of it and we treat them badly to boot. A mushroom managed organisation is typically one where management communication is either very poor or non-existent and where fear rules and where employees will not make decisions but refer them back to the family, who, in turn, will find their time consumed with making petty day to day decisions. I have seen this happen and family members complain about it but are still unwilling to let go and, sometimes, even blame the employees for not being decisive enough. It comes down to trust. We don't or shouldn't employ good people to tell them what to do. We should employ them to advise us on what to do, otherwise we don't get their full potential. Unlocking this can make a massive difference to company performance and efficiency and allows senior management and the family to focus on more strategic matters. Otherwise, we end up with micro-management by the family with all decisions coming back to the family or not being made at all.

Written business plans are static things. They are a picture in time of where the authors feel the business is and where its future lies. The business will naturally evolve and bend in response to the ebbs and flows of business life regardless of the business plan. It is a natural process. Accordingly, before we start the planning process, we need to agree amongst the family what we mean by a successful family business. This means identifying the personal objectives of the family, and individuals within the family may have different views on doing this and comparing these to corporate objectives.

5. Setting the business objectives

It does not matter at what stage in the company's life we are at when it comes to setting objectives. The original objectives in setting up the business may have changed, failed or have been accomplished. Refreshing the corporate objectives should be a regular thing. This does not mean that we change strategic direction every five minutes but that we review our objectives - if we have any that is - on a periodic basis. Quite often in family and owner managed businesses the objectives are unwritten and assumed and they are usually associated with meeting a lifestyle for the owners. There is nothing wrong with this of course and, probably, most small businesses were set up with this financial objective in mind rather than that of conquering the world. Of course, there are exceptions such as not for profit businesses in the voluntary sector that are set up to meet a social or community need. Nevertheless, they must be financially stable and able to remunerate staff to a satisfactory level.

So, we are at a point where we would like to set or re-establish our objectives as part of our forward thinking and strategic planning. As a family or owner managed business there are two sets of objectives to consider.

- Personal or Life objectives
- Corporate objectives

The best way of setting objectives is through a Strategic Workshop. This should involve those people who have real influence on the determination of future strategy and who benefit financially either through reward or employment. These are likely to be owners and directors rather than non-decision-making family members. Both sets of objectives can influence each other. This is because businesses are started for a variety of reasons including:

- The founder has identified a gap in the market for a product or service that he or she has developed.
- The founder has started a business out of one in which he or she was previously employed
- The founder used redundancy pay to create a business in order to be employed.
- The founder was unemployed and the only way to earn a living was to start a business
- The founder always aspired to own and manage a business

Of course, this may not be a first-generation business. It could well be that the objectives of the current owners and managers differ to that of the founder(s). Typical situations are:

- The current family members managing the business are only doing so at the behest of their parents but either may not be the most appropriate makers, or their heart is elsewhere or both.
- They have ambitions to take the business to a different place.
- They want to follow in their parents' footsteps.

- They want to grow the business and possibly sell or build an empire.
- They want to build or secure the business for inheritance by their children.
- Their children are unlikely to come into the business due to their young age or because the current generation does not have children.

If there is more than one generation in the business, it may be that there are differing views regarding the aims and objects of the company and its future strategy. This is usually a source of potential conflict and can be difficult to resolve depending upon the personal relationship between the various family members and their willingness to compromise or accept change. It is also determined by the influence of the majority shareholder(s). Quite often this is the founder who may also have a seat on the board or may have influence through family members of the board. Sometimes these family members can be persuasive in setting the course of the business. Sometimes they can be restrictive or, even, destructive.

Accordingly, compiling a business plan is not necessarily as straight forward as in a non-family corporate organisation. Not only do we have management and shareholders to consider; we have to take into account family members, whether they be shareholders, spouses or relatives. It is important for family directors and owners to clarify, or, even, think about their life objectives and how that might sit with the aims of the business. The corporate objectives may be the ones that will facilitate the realisation of these personal objectives. The best way of doing this is through the Strategic Workshop.

6. The Strategic Workshop

It is usually best if this is facilitated by a third party such as an advisor rather than a family member. This is the most diplomatic way of keeping everyone focused and avoids people going off at a tangent or unnecessary unrelated conversation about family issues which can rapidly turn into disagreement and even argument. If it is a family member then it should be someone either experienced in facilitation or who has the respect of others to carry out the task. If it is family run, then we must avoid a free for all conversation similar to a family social gathering. This must strictly be a disciplined and structured event. Family objectives, as previously stated may be either to grow or maintain a financial model that maintains a lifestyle and nothing more. In many cases families do not clearly define their objectives when setting up a business.

Using a flip chart or other media, the facilitator should use one page per family member and have two columns: the left side being personal objectives and the right being corporate ones. This allows us to compare the two lists of objectives for each individual. It is usually best if everyone lists their personal objectives first. It is important for everyone to be honest and not be influenced by other family members or to feel that they have to say what might please the founders or parents. Some of the personal objectives I have seen range from the aesthetic to the mercenary and have included making sufficient money to carry out voluntary work in a developing country, building a business that can be handed down through generations, making a difference in the community and making enough money to retire to a home overseas. Corporate objectives could be how the family members see the business in the future taking into consideration things such as the level of growth, the company's potential position and reputation in the market, the level of profit and financial sustainability as well its size, structure, and product range. This is visionary stuff to some degree, but we should be as specific as possible and go beyond those vague mission statements like 'to be the leading provider in the market' or 'to be the number one fashion designer in the country' as, although these sound worthwhile they are difficult to translate into actions. We all need a vision. We all need to be going somewhere but we need to decide and understand where that 'somewhere' is. It our choice as citizens of this planet. Whether we get there is another matter.

Having completed both life and corporate objectives we should summarise both as we are likely to find that many are shared. We then need to reconcile the two to see if the corporate objectives allow us to fulfil our life ones and if the life objectives hinder or influence the corporate ones. From this we can then focus on agreeing the corporate objectives of the company. These should be realistic and pragmatic as much as possible. Having defined our objectives, we then need to visualise the business model as it should be in, say, three to five years' time.

6.1. Personal objectives

Each participant in the workshop should be asked to identify their personal objectives in life, regardless of the business. These may range from starting and looking after a family to providing a social or community need or simply making enough money to spend the rest of their lives playing golf on the Algarve in Portugal. Accordingly, the business is here to provide the finances to support these objectives. You may find that some participants have a personal objective that is also a corporate one in that they want to create a service or product that will make a name or even make them famous. So, their personal and corporate objectives are the same, or so it would seem. It is likely that want they really want is to make a personal impact upon the world, whether that be the commercial world or the real world. There may be someone who wants to take time out from the business at some point to fulfill a personal project or even limit their life in the family to a specific term.

If you are in the media business, it may be that you want to influence the general public or be a particular source of information. Again, these may be similar to corporate objectives. We need to drill down deep to understand personal objectives. If these cannot be satisfied by the finances or success provided by the business, then we may have an issue with motivation and commitment. Against each participant we should list their personal objectives. You might find the results surprising. You may also find that some are similar and some a million miles away from each other. You may find some that potentially could clash with the interests of the business. You will also find that some will have not really thought about their personal objectives in life as many people tend to 'go with the flow ' in life and do not think long term. There is not anything necessarily wrong with this and it is not the place of the facilitator to be judgmental. Nevertheless, we need to determine what individuals want out of the business from a personal perspective. It may well be that it is simply a job that enables them to pay the bills.

So, in summary, you will find that some business owners will have personal objectives distinct from corporate ones and that the business is there to facilitate a lifestyle and achieve personal objectives. You will find that with others their personal and corporate are the same or very closely intertwined. They will not necessarily be able differentiate between the two. Their personal objectives may include a desire to build and sell the business, not necessarily for personal gain on its own but to go on to do another project. In other words, the business is just a means to an end.

6.2. Corporate objectives

If we have the personal objectives written down on one side of the white board, the other side should list the corporate objectives as defined or understood by each participant. We should try to go beyond the obvious such as 'grow the business', 'maximise profits' etc., but think about products, services and markets and about what value the business might be adding to its sector, the community, and the economy.

- Is our family business going to make a real difference in the sector it serves?
- Are we creating or developing something new?
- Do we want a build a reputation for quality/innovation/financial success/reliability/market leadership/product or service reliability etc.?

- Do we want to build and exit or hand down through the family?
- Do we need a succession plan to manage the business in the future?

It is worth thinking about the style of business we want. Is it a lifestyle business to meet the financial needs of the family or is it an entity in its own right with family as equal beneficiaries alongside other stakeholders (other shareholders, investors, the bank, employees, directors etc.)? One of the most fundamental questions to consider at this point is whether we actually and really want to grow the business and, if so, to what degree. The business may have settled on a comfortable plateau generating modest enough profits to support the family lifestyle.

There are risks in growth and we need to ask ourselves whether we want to take those risks. Having said that, businesses cannot stand still. Markets, products and technology continually change, and the old adage is true in business in that we have to more forward simply to stand still. In business there is always natural erosion. Customers go away to competitors, their demands for our services change, they employ new people who look elsewhere for their suppliers, technology changes rapidly, fashions continually change and evolve, customers and suppliers go bust, our suppliers and business partners are no longer dependable and so the list goes on. The market or community that any business lives in is a dynamic and fluid thing that continually changes and sometimes declines. We can never be complacent and assume that what went before will happen again. Too much dependence on too few customers can lead to disaster. The fact that we have a good relationship with a major customer today does not mean that we will have one tomorrow. Of course, there exceptions to this as there always are. Businesses that have been set up based on long term contracts with public sector organisations are an example. However, it may be that the life of the business is determined by the length of the contract.

At this stage we are not looking to develop our corporate strategy. We simply want to understand what each participant in the workshop believes our corporate objectives to be or what they feel they should be (what we would like to achieve rather than how we are going to achieve it).

Having listed both personal and corporate objectives alongside each other we need to reconcile the two

6.3. Reconciliation of objectives

It is essential that both personal and corporate objectives are aligned in some way. This may mean that the corporate objectives enable the personal ones to happen or that both personal and corporate are similar, if not the same. We should go through each of the personal objectives line by line, person by person to identify where there might be a conflict or where the corporate ones do meet personal objectives. We need to discuss and modify the corporate objectives until they are aligned to the personal ones. At the end of the day the personal objectives are the most important in that if they cannot be met through the business then we have lost the principal incentive for individuals to achieve corporate objectives. We also need to consider whether or how the corporate objectives can enable personal objectives to be achieved. We should now agree and list the corporate objectives in preparation for building our family business strategy.

Family Business Matters

7. Developing our strategy

There are several stages involved in developing our strategy. These include setting our objectives, the methods of achievement, its management and the means of measuring its progress and success.

7.1. Achieving the strategic objectives

The purpose of this stage is to determine how the objectives will be met. We need to consider life three to five years hence and build ourselves a model of how we think the business should look in terms of products or services, turnover, structure, etc. We must think at a high level in terms of scale and size. At this stage these are only working numbers. The detail will come later. Many business managers are reluctant to work with high level numbers. Quite often the financial forecasts are compiled by the accountant on a 'bottom up' basis. That is when we take previous year's performance and extend them. This is not the way to strategically develop the business and financial forecasts. We must put ourselves in a forward position and if we like where we are we then must determine how to get there; what steps to take; what changes to make.

We need to think carefully about our products and services and the market we operate in. It is worth considering the .likely life of our current offering. It may be that some of our products or services either need to be updated or replaced. We should try to get an understanding of where we are in our particular market. Successful businesses know their market well because they are in touch with it through networking, seminars, conferences, exhibitions and research. They also talk to business managers within the supply chain and even competitors. Sadly, too many leaders of small businesses are not in touch with the market because they 'do not have the time'. They are too busy doing the day job to think about the future. To understand the market we serve we have to be in it, breathing it, living it. Hopefully at the workshop there is at least one person with this knowledge. If not, then one of our first actions must be to commission someone to fulfil this role. Unfortunately, it is likely to be a slow burn. Knowledge will grow gradually and eventually become embedded into the culture and intellectual property of the business. Avoid the 'quick fix such as engaging a firm of researchers. This knowledge needs to be home grown. If you do not have this knowledge in house, then we can still proceed with the caveat that market insight needs to be gained or improved. This should be one of your strategic objectives and someone should be actioned to be the owner of the initiative.

The decisions regarding products and services may be aspirational to some degree and may require more discussion and research before finalisation. We should not worry unduly over this as all we are trying to do is set the general direction of the business. Many companies I have worked with have been founded on a good idea. That is the founder of the business has something in mind which they think the market will want, or it is something that the founder is passionate about and assumes that there are potential customers out there. Sometimes this works but more often than not it does not. The number of startups that fail is high. In Europe 82% of first-time entrepreneurs eventually fail and 50% of start business collapse within three years. The figures in the USA are not dissimilar. 21.5% fail within the first year and 50% by year three. These are not encouraging statistics if you are thinking of starting up in business. This is despite the huge amount of state support given to start-ups through incubation units, grants, soft loans etc. Yet, government after government place great emphasis on start-ups as the way to either grow or recover an economy. Admittedly, many of these businesses will have failed due to management or finance issues. Nevertheless, when we are considering new products and services and the life span of the existing product range we need to build confidence that there is, or will be, market demand.

One way of checking market demand is to review what our competitors or other companies are doing. It could be that there is a role model out there. I have used this approach in the past when planning a business and did it successfully when I ran Silver Cross Prams Ltd in the North of England. The company was quite old fashioned in its thinking and the product range had become quite dated. I found a market leader and reviewed their offering and customer service. We then copied this but added the value of the Silver Cross brand, which dated back to the nineteenth century, and made additional features to our customer offering and customer experience. So, you identify someone who is leading the market and basically follow the leader by replicating what they do, where you can, but endeavor to do it better and eventually overtake them.

Once it is agreed in which direction we are going with products and services, we need to scale the business, initially in terms of potential revenue streams for each product, project or service line. Do not have too many lines; five or six is about right, but certainly no more than ten. Against each line we need to estimate the cost of sales. If you are in a service industry such as accounting or other professional service, then it is likely that you will not have a cost of sales line and if you do it will be so small as to be insignificant. Cost of sales can be defined in different ways depending on your business and the view of your accountant. It is sometimes referred to as the variable cost, particularly in manufacturing and in these cases includes both materials and labour. This goes back to the days when labour was a directly variable cost as factory employees were often paid on piecework; that is paid for pieces produced. These days labour is more of a semi-fixed cost, particularly in small businesses. Larger corporates sometimes employ temporary staff or use staff on what are known as 'zero hour contracts' where they can flex the hours employed. You should use whatever is currently in use or best understood in your own business for this exercise. Generally, it is the cost incurred to get the sale and will include buying the raw materials or products, distribution and, in some manufacturing companies, the cost of the labour to produce the goods. From this we can estimate or future gross margin. We now need to look at our overhead and consider where this might increase, assuming we are going for growth. We may need extra sales or marketing resource to generate the additional sales, or we may need to invest more in e-commerce or administration. We may also need additional technical or professional skills. From this we can, of course, estimate projected profit levels. We will probably need to play around with the figures until we come up with a broad brush financial a model.

The results from the workshop should be that we have a definitive picture of what we believe the business could look like in terms of structure, products, services and market and we will have some rough-cut financial projections. These are sufficient to give us some strategic direction and it is important that all the participants in the workshop walk away in agreement. The follow up is in developing the detail and we can be certain that there will be modifications as our ideas and aspirations are tested more thoroughly through discussion and research. When this is complete it can be embodied in a business plan and like all business plans should be shared with the staff; the very people who are employed to deliver it.

7.2. Building the future business model

The future business model we create will become the basis for the structure of our business plan. In the workshop we are working at a high level so it is very much top down not bottom up. We should avoid getting into too much detail. That can come later. It is more important that we work with numbers and estimates and our existing knowledge of the market we serve. If we cannot work at this level then there is a failing in our understanding of the market and our grasp of the business.

We firstly need to agree on whether we are looking for growth. There is no point in setting out on a growth strategy if we do not have the personal appetite for it. Growth invariably means some form of change in what we do and how we do it. It is likely to require additional resource and there are likely to be cost implications. For example we may have to invest in people and fixed assets as well as materials and consumables and other working capital.

We have already agreed on the products or services we intend to provide and where we may want to diversify or extend the range. For example: are we going to focus on organic growth or consider other market opportunities? This may have an impact on product development and research as well as marketing and staffing. Having agreed, in broad terms, the range of potential services, we should also agree on which geographical markets we believe offer realistic opportunities if we are going for growth. This, of course, depends upon the nature of the business and whether it serves a local need or a wider one including international trading. If it is an internet-based business or one that sells both directly and on-line then it could well serve a global market, depending on the nature of the product of course and the costs of shipping the product. If you are considering new geographical markets then err on the side of caution in terms of expansion. Expansion into foreign countries can sometimes be the graveyard of many companies. However, at this stage if we believe there are opportunities in a specific country we simply caveat this by stating that it will be subject to further research, or, it may well be that we have knowledge and experience of the country concerned to make this a particular target.

Conversely it is important to consider those products, services or markets that we might want to pull out of due to poor margins, market decline or product ageing. This can be done strategically on a phased basis if appropriate and should be planned with a view to minimising costs and impact upon the remaining business and customer relationships. Pulling out of poor performing markets can often result in overall margin improvement in the business. One option is to price ourselves out of the market. For example, when I was running Silver Cross Prams, one of our most significant and iconic products was the traditional steel bodied pram that one sees in old movies these days. The production of these was mixed up with the manufacture of other modern prams and buggies. However, sales of these traditional prams had been in decline for a number of years apart from Scandinavia where they were popular as they kept out the cold and the large wheels negotiated well in the snow. I carried out a cost review including timing the production. It was clear that margins were not good and had a negative impact on the profit line. We decided to extract from the market. The product was moved from mainline production into a dedicated unit with its own flow line. This incurred little capital expenditure as it mainly involved moving existing equipment and tools to a new location. I doubled the price of the product and put out some low-cost marketing and editorial saying that this product line may be discontinued. Sales increased for a while and with the new flow line we made healthy margins and the over recovery of overhead. This lasted for nearly 12 months until sales went back into decline. With the higher price we still made a modest profit.

Having agreed on the above we now need to estimate or 'guesstimate' the potential revenue against each market and product grouping. This should not be in detail with nothing more than about 5/10 sales lines and should be on an annual basis. At this stage these are merely aspiration although we should have some degree of confidence that the estimates are reasonable. The next step is to plug in the costs. These may or may not increase in line with increased sales, although if you are in manufacturing or construction then there may be a proportional increase in material, component and subcontract costs. It may be that we expect to see an improvement in gross margins, in which case we can set targets such as a percentage improvement each year. Taking existing overheads as a starting point we need to make estimates of increased costs in areas such as staff, marketing and other overheads. We can quickly build a broad-brush financial model of how we see the company's potential financial performance over the next three years. At this point a break in the workshop can be useful to give people time to reflect.

Having developed a future business model, the next, and most important step is to determine how we get there; the things that need to be done and resources that need to be employed, hired or bought. Again, we do these in broad terms at this stage, such as 'we need to improve our digital and social media marketing', or 'we need to invest in certain technology or plant and equipment', or 'we need to employ a sales director', 'we need to develop our product range further', etc. We then allocate these tasks out so that we can come up with more detailed plans of action on each.

We now have a broad-brush plan with actions for people to complete. When these are done, we can start to build a more detailed plan and forecasts. These are bound to differ to some degree to our original 'guesstimates', but we have managed to focus, and it is remarkable what can be achieved in a short period of time. Follow up is the key to maintain the impetus we have started, otherwise day to day matters will consume our time at the expense of the future.

8. The family business plan

One of the understandable concerns that many managers have about compiling business plans is that it can be a time-consuming process that can detract them from running the business. The other issue is that many owner managers believe there is no need for a business plan as a formal thing as they know where the enterprise is going and the plan is 'in my head', as one managing director once told me. It was in no one else's and that was the problem.

Business planning should not be a one-off exercise. It is, to some extent, an ongoing process. It can be likened to a campaign of war. The outline strategy is agreed, and the initial attack formulated in detail. The course of the war may very much depend upon the outcome of this initial foray. We then start to work of the battle plan for each stage of the war in more detail. Nevertheless, we will experience success and failure. We will move forward and sometimes retreat or hold fire. Therefore, our planning needs to be flexible and responsive to the circumstances as they occur whilst endeavoring to maintain our overall strategy, but even this may have to be flexed. In a war as in business we do not know what the enemy has planned or how this plan might be executed. We do not know they will behave or respond to our own strategy and campaign. However, in our war the enemy is not just the opponent or opponents but could be the weather (many a battle has been lost or won due to the weather - the battles at Agincourt and Waterloo were influenced by the weather). It could also be the home economy and our ability to sustain armaments production and food supply. It could be the willingness of the people to support a war campaign in which they see no benefit. In business our 'enemies' include the competition; the economy, both in our own country and the countries we trade with; the marketplaces and the forces and trends within it; the access to cash to sustain the campaign, including bank support and growth capital, and the availability of human resource with the appropriate skills and experience to help us deliver the strategy and win the war. All these facets need to be considered in our planning process.

Having agreed on our corporate business model we now develop the means of achieving it and the various steps and actions that must be taken. Accordingly, our plan should be action based and include the empowerment and involvement of all staff, to a greater or lesser degree depending upon their role. Some staff, not just because they happen to be managers, but because their role in the organisation or their particular skills set is relevant and key to achieving the plan need to be involved with its development. However, we should not focus too much on the written word. We are not writing a novel. We need to convey our plans to those who will deliver it in the form of the means of achieving the objectives we have set ourselves. This can be done through workshops and briefings. Firstly, we need to address each of the objectives we have set ourselves line by line. If we are going for growth there are different routes.

8.1. Organic growth.

We are confident that there is a market for our products, either because we have existing knowledge of the market and the competition, or because we have carried out or commissioned some research. Many small businesses depend on repeat business and are usually proud of the fact. They see no need for active marketing and selling because the sales orders are coming in anyway or because it is traditionally not necessary in their particular market sector. There can also be a degree of complacency in that the level of revenue is sufficient to meet the lifestyle objectives of the owners so why bother investing in marketing and selling? Another factor is a lack of marketing and selling skills or function in the organisation.

I have often witnessed companies who have experienced a decline in sales embark upon a cost cutting exercise, which, of course is a natural and sensible response. What is less sensible is that they very often cut out all marketing activity and reduce their sales team. One managing director one told me 'We haven't got the sales so I can't afford to employ sales staff!'. The other area usually to be cut is training. If we are going to grow the business we have to invest in sales and marketing. This may not necessarily mean rushing off to the nearest recruitment agency but a realignment of roles and responsibilities in the management team. Quite often the best person to lead the sales drive is the managing director. The managing director knows the business well but more importantly can make contractual decisions such as margins and discounts where the sales manager might have to report back. Also the very fact that the business leader is meeting customers makes a big impression.

Organic growth can be a lower risk option providing there is the opportunity for growth in the market the company serves. This can be that the market itself is growing or that the company's share of it is actually quite small. However, these facts alone are not sufficient for us to be confident of success. If we have the right structure we can afford to let the managing director loose in the market place and focus on business development whilst the management team manage the day to day stuff, and, in many cases in my experience they will do it more effectively, without the continual presence and possible interference of the CEO.

8.2. Growth through diversification.

In the agricultural industry in the UK small family-owned farms have seen a decline in revenue in traditional farming. They have compensated through diversification. This has sometimes, for example, been a move from dairy farming to arable or market vegetables. It has sometimes been the setting up of new but related enterprise such as the dairy farmer making and selling yoghurt and cheese; in other words, moving up the supply chain. Other examples are the establishment of a cafe or farm shop. These new diversified enterprises use the existing resources (the land and people), the assets of machinery and premises and the inherent skills of the people. So, in our business we may have assets, including people, that are underutilized along with skills that could be applied to different products or services. It may be that we have to import a specialist from the proposed new sector to either advise, or, more likely, lead the diversification. If we set up a diversified product line it is essential that we understand the costs it and treat it as a separate cost centre in order to monitor and manage margins and the success of the enterprise.

8.3. Strategic Growth

Strategic growth means thinking differently about how we grow the business. It could mean making some very bold decisions about the structure of the business, its ownership and future direction. The family must consider that they may be going into an environment where they have less control over the destiny of the business and its impact on the family.

Loss of ownership has to be balanced against the financial gains a new owner might bring. I see many examples where owner managers cling on to shares as if they were gold pieces and are reticent to see any dilution of their shareholding. Shares mean very little if the company is never to be sold. Of course, there are dividends to consider, but how many small family or owner managed businesses pay out regular substantial dividends? Nevertheless, many people see having shares in a business as being something of importance and value.

These factors need to be considered very seriously when considering strategic growth. My interpretation of strategic growth in a family business environment involves changing the structure and ownership of the business. The various means of strategic growth include:

- Acquisitions and Mergers
- Joint ventures

- Strategic partnerships

8.3.1. Acquisitions & Mergers

Family businesses are not normally acquisitive. Many acquisitions fail, despite comprehensive, and usually very expensive, due diligence by accountants and lawyers who often fail to pick up the key issues of the business being acquired, as their approach is based upon prescriptive check lists. I recall one acquisition of a large manufacturing company I was working on. Due diligence was carried out by one of the top four accounting firms who valued the stock at £750,000. In reality the stock was worthless as you could not make one product out of it. I calculated that I would have to spend another £1.5m to make complete products and by then some of the product designs might have gone out of date. To carry out due diligence you have to understand the way a business runs.

One of the biggest causes of acquisition failure is the difference in culture between the acquirer and the acquired. In a family business the culture is well ingrained and embedded because it is that of the family. To incorporate the culture of another business into a family business is likely to be extremely arduous and difficult. It is more than likely to be worse if is another family business that is being acquired. The only way to make it succeed is to impose the acquirer's culture. If you look at the way the larger accountancy firms have grown you can see that the acquirer is the one that imposes the culture. I was with Coopers and Lybrand when there was a 'merge over' by Price Waterhouse. Very quickly the culture in the Coopers & Lybrand offices became that of the dominant partner, Price Waterhouse, despite Coopers & Lybrand having a long a strong history and its own identity.

In my experience acquisitions can be a way to achieve more rapid growth but in the family context we need to tread carefully and ensure that acquisitions fit the values ethics and culture of the acquirer.

If the family company believes that its future growth has to be through acquisition then a Buy and Build strategy could be appropriate. In effect we use the family business as the holding company or create a holding or mother company and endeavor to build a portfolio business. This means that imposition of the culture of the holding company is less critical. We can allow the acquired businesses to maintain their own culture to some degree, although there would be some element of modification or adjustment to comply with the overall values and objectives of the mother company.

8.3.2. Joint ventures

Joint ventures ('JVs') can work particularly well if we are looking to expand into new geographical markets. They are a lower risk than an outright acquisition. In a JV we typically set up a new company in which both parties have a stake. This is usually 50:50 but could be some other formula to suit the engaging partners. However, with a JV there must be a real willingness by both parties to make it work. In addition, the JV will need financing and management. The objectives of the JV need to be very clearly defined and sufficient resource, time and effort will need to be employed to make it work. The risk is that without enough time and attention it will fail.

8.3.3. Strategic partnerships

Strategic partnerships or alliances are easier to set up than JVs and do not require the same level of investment, if any. It is usually a collaboration on marketing and business development with, typically, cross border alliances. However, real effort must be made by both partners to make them work. All too often alliances are made and not followed through.

To have a strategic alliance we must have common goals or aims and serve related markets. An example of a strategic alliance could be one between your company and a distributor or sales agency; that you agree to work together on a marketing and sales campaign is a specific geographical region or marketplace. Another example could between you and a business within your supply chain or someone providing a service or product that can be bolted on to yours.

8.3.4. *Memorandum of Understanding*

A memorandum of understanding ('MOU') is a good way of forming an initial relationship with a partner enterprise or business without the legal entanglement of a JV or the exclusivity of a strategic alliance. It is a commitment on the part of both participants to work together for mutual benefit. This could be the sharing of market information, joint events, cross referral of business where one party does not have the capacity, products or resources. It could be that the two parties already have a relationship as supplier and customer and there is a market and cost/process advantage in working together to secure new business ahead of the competition.

9. Culture

In my experience it is the culture of an organisation that can determine future success or failure. All too often I have seen the culture of fear management, in both family and non-family businesses, whereby employees are afraid of making decisions due to the potential consequences of getting it wrong.

The culture of an organisation can be influenced by many factors but it is the leader or leadership of the business that has the biggest influence. Changing the culture is impossible to achieve without the leadership changing behaviour or style of management or if the leadership is replaced. Other influential factors include the historical development of the enterprise, the views of employees, particularly the culture of the community from which the workforce stems, as well as their socio-economic makeup, and, also, the market that the company serves and its influence on behaviour. For example, recruitment or other sales-based organisations can be aggressive and fast-moving sectors requiring people, usually young, who aspire to earn high levels of remuneration, are highly incentivised and, in return, expected to work tenaciously. They often must work in a marketplace of cold calling and a non-receptive customer base. They probably enjoy their social life at the same pace and if you visit the bars around certain parts of the city of London on a Friday evening after office hours you will see them flushed with successes of their week.

Many consultants talk about changing culture, but why would you want to do that if is not detrimental to the smooth running and success of the enterprise? Trying to change the culture of a family business is a daunting task anyway and is often impossible unless there is succession in terms of leadership. A non-family member trying to change culture in a family business can be onto a non-starter and could face resentment from the family. As a consequence, most do not even try. Nor should they. The change in culture must come from the family, but how can a family change its values and ethics and the way it behaves: with great difficulty I would imagine.

So why would we need to change culture in a family business? We only need to change culture if the existing one is detrimental to the success of their business. However, family members are often unlikely to recognise if this is the case and trying to change the culture of a family business is, in reality, an attempt to change behaviour of the family itself. An impossible task in most cases. The only way to do it is by removing the family from senior executive positions or reducing their participation in the affairs of the business. Families will only do this if:

- They have become tired of running the business and want to move on or retire
- They recognise that they do not have the skills to manage the business under current circumstances.
- They may be second or third generation and never really wanted to be in the business.

- There may not be a successor from within the family.
- An equity investor such as a private equity firm may make it conditional that a new business leader is introduced.

We may not be able to radically change the culture of a family business because of the personalities involved but we can modify behaviour if this is necessary to achieve corporate objectives.

There are three ways of doing this:

- Empowering middle management and staff to make decisions without reference to family members of management.
- Modifying the way we communicate with staff so that it is more participative.
- Identifying a family member such as an incoming manager who is keen to adopt change and encouraging and enveloping them.

There are occasions when an incoming family member is keen replace what has gone before and modernise the business. Sometimes for the sake of it to make an impression or create a business fashioned in a model that reflects the person, but often because a real need for change has been identified.

10. Shareholding

Some years ago. I met with a family business in the North West of England. The 'family' in fact comprised three brothers. They had all worked in the automotive industry and had identified a gap in the market which they felt they had the skills to fill. To them it was an opportunity to build a business supplying a particular much needed component. They were all technically experienced but had little, if any, management experience, although they knew the business they were in. They knew who the likely customers would be and had already made some enquiries that gave them sufficient confidence that this enterprise would work. So, they met together in pub one night and, with great excitement decided to embark upon this great adventure with visions of success and wealth in their minds.

Being three brothers it made sense to split the shareholding of the business three ways. They registered it accordingly at Companies House. Why wouldn't they? There was no need for any legal agreement. The business kicked off and was a success. Twenty years passed and the world changed. The automotive sector was struggling. Nevertheless, the company was holding up, but they were all twenty years older and now seemed a good time to sell. There was some interest in buying the business with a very attractive financial offer when they approached me, but there was a problem. The eldest brother had disappeared. He had left his wife and gone off to Thailand to 'find himself' and nobody had any idea exactly where he was; probably painting pictures on a beach somewhere. He had deserted both family and friends. He did not exist. Except he did exist as a 33% shareholder of business that was on the brink of being sold. The buyers wanted control and they could not get that whilst a significant shareholder could not be found. The alternative was to put the company into liquidation, which as directors they could do unless there was an objection by the majority of shareholders, in which case they would get nothing for the business as it would be bought out of liquidation.

They decided to keep on trading and not retire much to the chagrin of their respective families.

I have seen other cases where shares get diluted through the family and through more than one generation. It all seems very nice and equitable at the time but then we find we have given away a significant proportion of voting shares and the future can be dependent upon old Aunt May who inherited shares from her deceased husband and who has no interest in the business whatsoever having retired to a bungalow at the seaside with the shares certificate resting innocuously at the bottom of a bedroom cabinet drawer, unseen and forgotten.

Of course, when the business is handed down through generations shares can become diluted as they are distributed by parents to children, and this can become a real problem when issues arise in the company requiring shareholder agreement and can potentially lead to a loss of control on the part of shareholders who are executive directors in the business. Some family business owners will reduce the risk of this by putting shares into trusts or by limiting the distribution of shares through a shareholders' agreement.

Accordingly, when allocating shares within the family, priority should be given to those working in the business. However, if one sibling is working in the business and in receipt of some equity you may find that the others expect to be treated in a compatible fashion despite having no involvement in the business and no influence over its future and success. I have seen situations where a family member working in the business was given a significant shareholding. The other sibling was not involved in the business at all but was nevertheless very bitter that he did not receive any shares. To be told that he would benefit when the parents died was not the answer he was looking for, particularly as his parents were only in their 50s and had no funeral plans. The solution to situations like these is to consider giving them a lower level of shares, or, preferably, non-voting shares which yield some dividends. Ideally the terms of acquiring shares or shares distribution should be identified when the business is first set up through a shareholders agreement.

11. Communication

Of course, any activity that involves more than one person requires communication of some sort. The world is driven by words. However, language is often misconstrued or interpreted wrongly. Sometimes the words and expressions we use don't fully convey what we really mean or want to say. In this age of succinct emails and text messages the true intention of the message is not always conveyed accurately. The accuracy of the information we contain in any communication is vital if we want a particular response, action or result. In the main there are two forms of communication – one way and two way. In business we use both. In a family business the way we communicate reflects what we are as a family and is the culture of the organisation. Culture is all about communication and behaviour, but most of all communication. The arts are nothing more than a means of communicating with us with the artists interpretations through paintings, the music we hear that inspires or reflects, the literature we read, the theatre, the cinema etc. They drive the culture of a community. Likewise, in business the culture of the organisation is the way it communicates and through that the way it behaves.

But communication can be done through actions and the way we behave we each other. Each time we engage with someone we communicate. The best way to engage with employees therefore is to involve them in the business and its decision making processes, to counsel them and to allow them to participate in the things that drive the enterprise.

11.1. Sunday Lunch Syndrome.

The Sunday Lunch Syndrome has already been referred to. This ability for the family to change its mind after consultation offsite is one of the biggest causes of friction and frustration amongst non-family members. However, when you own a business you cannot walk away from it outside of work hours. It is your baby and a member of the family. It's a living breathing dynamic thing. Without your continual supervision and care, surely it will die, or least become very sick?

There is no way that a family business owner, or indeed any owner manager will be capable of totally switching off on a Friday night, and this can apply to employees who are dedicated to the business and take ownership and responsibility. Usually this means thinking about the business and returning to work with fresh ideas. Often, in a family business the decision to change is made outside office hours. Of course, this can be quite legitimate. If the family owns the business, why can they not decide or make changes outside the office? It is their business after all! Of course, they can, and they do. The critical thing is to differentiate between family business and the business.

11.2. The family v business differential.

Of course, in a family business personal agendas of family members can get mixed up with that of the business. But this can also be true of owner managed businesses. As long as businesses continue to be run by people and not robots then personal agendas will continue to influence the ways in which businesses are managed.

As family members in the business we have to put aside the family differential. This is hard to do. The family is the business and the business is the family. You cannot completely disentangle the two. A brother and a sister working together in a business are still siblings. A father does not stop being a parent to a child working in the company. Although it is hard to do we have to say 'outside of the office you are my brother: in the office you are my colleague'. It also means demonstrating to non-family members of staff that, with regard to the working environment, everyone has the same status as colleagues.

I recall the story of one family business owner who employed his son in the business. Unfortunately, despite much support and performance management, the son did not fulfil his role satisfactorily. His father felt he had no option but to dismiss him. He called him into his office and told him 'I am speaking to you now as your employer. Despite giving you full support this is not working and I am unfortunately going to have to let you go in the interests of the business.' The son was surprised as he was the owners son. How could this happen? The owner then addressed his son again 'now I am talking to you as your father. I understand you have lost your job. How can I help you?' The message here is that is the manager he had to make a commercial decision which was unrelated to his family relationship with the young man. Nevertheless, he was his father and as such had a real desire to help. Wherever, possible we need to differentiate between family and business.

11.2.1. The family executive board

We can extract the family agenda from the business by dealing with it separately through what are called family councils or family executive boards. These will be concerned with the business but through the eyes of the family. The council meeting agenda could typically include:

- Business strategy and objectives
- Corporate Governance matters
- Personal objectives of family members
- Roles and responsibilities of family members
- Succession planning
- Remuneration of family members
- Dividends
- Role of family members not in the business
- Share holding

- Retirement and succession matters

It is also a platform to discuss the business from a family perspective but in a more structured manner than informal gatherings of the family. In my experience it is usually better to get an external adviser to act as chair of the meeting. This could your trusted external accountant or other adviser such as a family business specialist. It could simply be someone outside the family you trust and respect and who is good at facilitation and the chairing of meetings.

This is not a meeting of the board of directors. They should carry on as normal. The family executive board could and, probably should, include members of the family who are not employed by the business but, nevertheless, have a vested in interest in the affairs of the company. These could include shareholders, spouses or other relatives whose livelihood depends in part or in whole upon the success of the business. Alternatively, they may simply be people who have an influence on the performance of the business or who's input is considered to be of value.

11.2.2. The family constitution

One of the outputs from the family council could be the creation of a family constitution. This document states the values that the family want to promote through the business as well as defining the way in which the family will engage with the business. For example, it could include rules regarding which family members can be employed in the business as well as details regarding their induction, training and development. It would typically also set out rules regarding remuneration and benefits to family members as well rules on the distribution of shares. One of the risks in family businesses, as mentioned previously, is the dilution of shares to such an extent that control by the executive members of the family can be lost.

One of the crucial areas to agree on is that of what constitutes the family and who can come into the business. Quite often family members can feel 'entitled' to a salaried position in the business. So is the family confined to the immediate one: for example the sons and daughters of the founders? Or do we include the children of the brothers and sisters of the founders – cousins. The other, more difficult position to consider is what happens if the son or daughter separates or divorces from their partner.

The best way is to change this from being complex to straight forward and simple. If we are acting in the interest of the business, and by doing this we are ultimately acting in the best interest of the family, then selection of family connected candidates to come into the business should be based on suitability and need. We don't create posts just to give someone a job. We don't employ someone from the family if they are clearly not the right person for the post. So some of the criteria for family members to come into the business could be:

- There is a position to be filled or created that is of value.
- The candidate is the right person for the job both in terms of capability and personality.
- The candidate is a family member who has the potential to be developed.

Of course, there is nothing wrong in positively discriminating towards family members, if that is what has been decided when compiling the family constitution. We are simply saying that this is a family business for the family and family members will be given preference during the selection of candidates for employment. Otherwise we might as well advertise vacancies on the open market and family members have to compete with everyone else. Our objective when setting up the business may have been to create something to 'hand down' to our children or for the extended family.

Nevertheless, there may come a situation when Auntie May calls to say that she would like to see her unemployed grandson or niece to be given a job. This is why the constitution is important as we can quote it. That does not mean we cannot vary if appropriate.

Another situation could arise if the two founders being co-habiting partners, either by marriage or consent, decide to separate. They may each have new partners and stepchildren come on the scene. If the two founders are still in the business then it may only be fair and equitable to include stepchildren although this is a difficult decision to make. A lot will depend upon the amicability of the relationship between the two founders. I worked with one family business which had this very situation. Husband and wife were divorced but both still worked in the business as shareholding directors with no other directors appointed. The meetings were held were mainly consumed with the two of them either arguing or making sarcastic comments about each other's new partners. There was clearly an element of jealousy on both parts and a reluctance to let go of that past relationship. The 'husband' wanted his new stepson to come into the business as he had just left college with no immediate prospects. The 'wife' responded with 'This is like throwing it in my face. You might as well bring HER into the business?' The only solution was, with some difficulty to agree on a constitution or formula for the future as to who could come into the business. We also agreed to appoint a third director from outside of the family. We chose someone mature enough to be able to calmly manage the situation. The stepson was not appointed but found a job elsewhere.

11.3. Engaging with staff.

All too often we find in business that communication can be a one-way process; a top-down approach from management, usually to keep employees up to date with what is going on. Of course there is nothing wrong with this bulletin type approach but, as management, we also want to find out what our employees are thinking and gauge their reactions to initiatives carried out by management. What we did at one family company in the South of England was to create a senior management team, we referred to as the SMT. This was comprised entirely of non-family members. They underwent some training on various topics including leadership, business planning, change management and financial management for non-financial managers. They met each month and one of them, based on a rota system, would report into the main board meeting on any issues or any initiatives they wanted the directors to consider. This worked really well and allowed the directors and family to focus on core strategic matters whilst the SMT dealt with the day to day operational side. It also meant there was a much better flow of information that was structured and documented and, of course, acted upon.

12. Take good care of my baby

Succession, or, usually, the lack of succession, is probably the biggest single issue amongst family businesses. A survey I carried on behalf of the UK government amongst 500 family businesses showed that the top issue was the matter of succession, or lack of it. The business is usually established by the founders with an expectation or hope that something has been created that will be inherited and that, assuming there are, or will be, children, they will succeed them. There are often dreams of creating a dynasty and, indeed, many household family business names can go back several generations. There are companies in the UK that are either family owned or managed that go back hundreds of years. Businesses such as Whitechapel Bell Foundry (1420), Shepherd Neame the brewers (1698), and Aspall Cyder (1728).

Of course, there are family business that do not last many generations and the statistics show that the majority do not go beyond the second generation. One of the main reasons for this is the lack of a suitable, or willing, successor, in addition to commercial factors such as loss of market share, general business decline etc.

Some second generation family firms fail because the children of the founders, who have taken on the mantle of running the business, either do not have adequate business acumen or talent or they are not as motivated or as passionate about the business as the founders. In some cases they will only be in the business because it is expected of them or because they are unable to find a suitable alternative career or job. Sometimes it is out of loyalty or love of a parent or parents and a desire to be with them. Parental pressure sometimes influences these decisions and sons and daughters will bow to this when, for example, they see mother of father struggling with ill health or where the parent has reached an age when he or she should really be enjoying the rewards of past endeavours and retiring or perhaps taking a back seat. For many children going into the family business can also be an easy option when choosing a career. For some it can be the worst option due to the nature of their relationship with parents or total disinterest in the business. This is often the case when the business has been established by someone coming out of a similar industry in a specialist sector that might be in decline or showing no growth but is something in which the founder has considerable experience, and, indeed may be passionate about. Of course getting founders to actually retire can be an issue in itself.

If succession is a major factor in the future success and sustainability of our family business then it is critical that we both consider the issues around succession and have a succession plan iUSAn which we have some confidence regarding its potential success.

The main issues around succession therefore are:

- Lack of a suitable successor from within the family.
- The risks of having a non-family successor.
- The expectations of potential successors.
- The willingness of retiring parents/founders to let go.

- The ability to trust the successor to secure the future of the business.

Of course, succession can be within the family or outside. If we go outside the family then is it really going to work? There are, of course, family friends, but this can be risky and relationships can be jeopardised if it does not work out and very often it does not.

12.1 Succession Planning

Succession Planning is one of the most important tasks to be carried out when building or managing a family business. From numerous surveys that have been carried out by various organizations including my own, succession, along with communication is seen as a major issue in family businesses. It is never too early to start succession planning. In fact, the best time to start is prior to setting up the business. However, to be realistic, this is probably not going to happen as it is unlikely to be the first thing in the mind of the founders. So, the best time to compile a succession plan is now.

12.2. The Succession Plan

A successful succession plan needs to cover a number of areas including who will own the business, now and in the future, the people who will be running the enterprise, what it will look like, and how it will be run. It needs to consider succession in terms of ownership, leadership and the business itself.

As described in section 10 the importance of determining the shareholding both now and in the future is critical to avoid dilution and potential loss of control. The succession plan should include who will be entitled to shares in the business and the type of shares. The plan cannot be written for you. It has to be owned and created by the family with input from professional advisers on the legal and financial implications and perhaps facilitated by a family business adviser.

The following is a guide as to what should be included in the plan.

12.2.1. Goals and objectives.

The corporate goals and objectives as outlined in our strategy need to be clearly defined in the plan.

This is what we will be expecting the successor to work toward.

12.2.2 Ownership.

As described previously it is important to agree who is entitled to participate in the ownership of the business in the future, in particular with regard to voting shares. Allowing children to give away shares ad nauseum without any control can lead to a total dilution of ownership, potentially away from the core family. The family may want to stipulate that a minimum percentage, say 51% or 76%, remains within the core family however that might be defined. Legal advice should be taken regarding potential matrimonial or civil partnership breakdowns and how this might influence the transfer of shares. It could be that voting shares are allocated to those working in the business. Overall it is better to be fairly rigid and strict on the allocation of shares.

12.2.3. Management.

We need to differentiate between management succession and succession of ownership. In terms of the future success of the business, management succession is the most critical. The plan should clearly define which members of the family can be considered for succession. For example, is succession confined to only the offspring of the founder or founders? Also what if the founders were a couple but had become separated or divorced. Will stepchildren be allowed to succeed into management, or even join the family firm? These are all matters that need to be thought about when drawing up the succession plan.

The other consideration is the issue of not having a successor from within the family. If the family wish the business to continue and have accepted that future leadership may come from someone outside the family, then we need to define:

a) How that person will be identified or recruited.
b) How they will be developed and integrated into the business.
c) What their relationship will be with the family.
d) Whether they will be allowed to participate as a shareholder and what type of shares and when.

With regard to the transfer of shares held by a non-family manager, then we have to consider whether those shares can be transferred by the shareholder upon exit from the business or the death of the shareholder. Normal practice would be for the shares to be returned to the family. Once again, it is essential to stress the need to control the distribution of shares due to potential long-term implications.

12.1.3. Timeline.

It is really important to set a timeline for our succession strategy. For example, if we know who the potential successors to leadership will be, we should determine when they will come into the business and on what basis. Their development into their prescribed role needs to be planned and, equally important, the date of retirement of their predecessor needs to be agreed. This may be phased but is essential that it is agreed otherwise we get into issues about not letting go, which is a classic problem in family businesses and is addressed in subsequent chapters.

12.2. Choosing the right successor

I recall one family business involved in the manufacture of telecommunication products who wanted to recruit a managing director to allow the founder to take a back seat. They knew a young man in their local community who was looking for a new position and could potentially fulfill the role. his parents were friends of theirs After all, they knew him personally so he could be trusted and they knew he had the same values and ethics of the family. He was offered the position and had joined the company with great enthusiasm when I met him. He was competent and appeared to be a good manager. However, there was one thing wrong; his relationship with the founder, who could not, would not, let go and treated him as he would treat his own son, with a continual commentary along the lines of 'that's not the way that I would do it'. The relationship broke down and the young man left. The founder picked up the reins again and was happy but the company had not moved forward one jot.

Choosing the right successor is always going to be difficult. There is never ever going to be any guarantee of successful succession. We all know how difficult it is to recruit people anyway. People can present very well in CVs and meetings and interviews but when it comes to taking them on board as employees, things often work out differently; sometimes for the better, sometimes for the worse. It is my view that recruiting people is one of the most difficult management tasks that one could imagine. In a lifetime of recruitment of key people, I can honestly say that I have never ever got it right 100% of the time. Of course, using recruitment agencies can be a nightmare. This is not entirely their fault, as these days they tend to work on a contingency or success fee basis. But at one time they were engaged under an exclusive basis with a retainer fee. So, what happens is that they will have a database of candidates they try to push and will send out their CVs based on a keyword search. So, for example you may be looking for an engineering surveyor. They will look through their database and find the word engineer and send out anyone's CV which has the word engineer in the body of the document. So, you may get Design Engineers, Mechanical Engineers; none of which are relevant. It is a 'Body Shop' approach which requires you to do all the work to find a suitable candidate. This can be both time consuming and a total waste of time.

In a family business it usually works better in terms of relationships and trust when a family member takes over. This may not always be the best solution for the business; or the family member may not be the best qualified, but we tend to trust family more than non-family. It can work with a non-family member leading the business if the family decides to disengage from managing the business themselves and either retain non-executive roles or simply remain as owners of the business with appointed directors. However, even when family members assume non-executive roles there can be tension. The biggest single issue for family business owners when appointing nonfamily successors is that of trust. So how do we overcome this and avoid, or, at least, minimise, the risk?

The way to gain trust is through experience and participation. The non-family successor has to feel a part of the family community in the business. That does not mean they have to attend the family barbecue or pick up the children from school (although some do or would like to). It means they must feel a part of the family as it pertains to the business and that means understanding the aims and objectives and aspirations of the family concerning the business. They must share the family values and ethics in relation to the organisation but also understand the personal aspirations of family members. It also means the family being inclusive and not coming up with surprises such as sudden changes in strategy discussed and agreed over a family gathering without consultation with the non-family directors of the business. The non-family successor should also be given time and some freedom to 'get on with the job'. He or she will gain experience in both leading the business and working in a relationship with the family. This will help to build confidence on the part of the family and with confidence comes trust.

Being a non-family CEO of a family business is not an easy ride. There can be feelings of exclusion, lack of trust and loneliness. This is particularly acute when the non-family successor is a more highly experienced business manager than family members active in the business, and, quite often this is the reason that he or she has been chosen. But it can also create resentment if an experienced outsider has been chosen over a less experienced family member. Typically, successors from within the family have little if no experience of business other than the family firm, certainly not in terms of management. However, this does not necessarily matter providing adequate training and development is in place. At one time it was quite normal for people to be employed in one firm for a considerable time if not a lifetime and progress to a senior level within the same firm where they had gained respect. The story of the young man joining the large corporate as tea boy and eventually becoming CEO or President is more than just fiction. It has happened.

Where there are concerns regarding an eternal successor it is worth having a mediator outside the business who both parties can relate to. This may be the 'family retainer' i.e., the family's lawyer or a perhaps a family business adviser or a trusted business friend of the family. This mediator should be able to take some of the emotion out of any concerns family members have and address issues of the external successor such as lack of communication and trust.

If we want succession within the family then we need to invest in it. This means developing and coaching the potential successors through a personal development plan not merely saying 'you need to come into the business Jack, (or Jill)'. The plan, ideally, should include some time outside the business either working for someone in a similar industry, although this does not really matter - it's the experience that counts, or, perhaps, working within the supply chain or, even, running their own small business for a while. If they run their own business it may not necessarily be a huge success and there is nothing wrong in this. It is worth exposing them to both success and failure. Assuming that we have a successor from within the family we first need to understand their motivation. Are they coming into the business because it is expected or because they want to?

This means a serious discussion about career options. Of course, family business owners like the thought of their children taking over and that is quite normal. Accordingly, if we want our children in the business then it must be put across as a serious, beneficial and enjoyable career option, not a role that has be taken up out of a sense of duty or family loyalty. The family successor may have doubts about their ability to run the business and whether they could do it in the same style as their parents. They may also have concerns about working for or with their members of the family. The sibling rivalry that pervaded in the family home is often transferred into the business. At the end of the day even if they are work colleagues they are still first and foremost, brothers and sisters as they were in the nursery and that is not going to change at the place of work.

One of the inherent risks in family succession is that we appoint the wrong person to take over as leader of the business. Quite often, in fact usually, it is the eldest sibling that is assumed to be the natural inheritor of the leadership role, a bit like royal or dynastic succession. The most appropriate successor is the one best suited to run the business not the one who might feel the most entitled or who the retiring parent considers to be the most entitled. This can be a hard decision, but it is a crucial one, both for the business and the family.

I recall one situation where a brother and sister were employed in a business owned by their parents. The father acted as chair. The son was the managing director. The daughter was the finance director. The company's performance was static. The daughter continually complained to her brother but nothing changed. The acrimony and disagreements were affecting both the business and the happiness of the family, which had always been a close one. Eventually it all came to a head when we held a family meeting. It was an explosive meeting with the father declaring that he would close it down unless something was sorted. I took the son to one side and he confessed that he did not want to work in the family business. He only did it out of family commitment and love of his father who expected it of him. He actually wanted to work in education, which was always his dream. I spoke to the daughter who said that her dream was to be managing director. We came back to the meeting and it was agreed that the son would be helped to fulfill his dream with a financial contribution from the family. The daughter became managing director; a new finance manager was appointed and the business began to grow more profitably. This close knit family became happy once again.

The next step is seriously to consider the suitability of the potential successor for the role of business leader or manager. We may have an enthusiastic potential successor from within the family but we can be fairly certain that they will not completely follow in mother's or father's footsteps. Their personality may be different. For example, the founder may be entrepreneurial and outgoing. The son or daughter may not. They may be more compliant and more of an organiser and perhaps a little introvert. If we expect this person to follow in the predecessor's footsteps it will fail, and it often does as quite often the founder or owner will assume that the son or daughter will follow on in the same style. That is unlikely to happen and the only way to make it happen is through constraint and limiting the scope of the incoming successor to manage affairs in their own way. This can end up with both the successor becoming disheartened and potentially the business not achieving its objectives or even failing. Lack of successful succession has caused financial failure in many businesses in my experience and has been the source of some of the turnaround work of my firm. Succession must be planned. There is no point in leaving the issue until the time has arrived when we need to consider who will follow on. It will be too late.

There was a family company in the U.K. where the founder, who was in his 60's was looking to retire. The business was hugely successful specialising in property development. The youngest son was in the business and the father was hopeful that he would follow in his footsteps. The father was concerned that the son did not have the same passion or enthusiasm as him and was less interested, and not so good in the project side of the business. I was asked to work out a personal development plan for the son.

When I interviewed both father and son it was apparent that they had different personalities and different styles of management and of the general way of doing things in the business. They did not share any common interest and did not socialise as father and son. The son once said to me "I'd love it if dad came out for a beer with me one night but he's not interested." Nevertheless, there was love and respect between the two of them. The father was very much the entrepreneur. He was more extrovert than the son and his style was very much to lead from the front, leaving a wake behind him for other people to sort. He was non-compliant and would often break the rules to achieve his objectives. He drove his car very fast and had numerous speeding fines. He was not interested in too much detail. His desk was cluttered though he knew where everything was. He could not be bothered to tidy it. But he had built a hugely successful business.

The son was the opposite. He was compliant and liked to work to a set of rules. His desk was immaculate, and he was well organised in everything he did. He particularly enjoyed administration and was keen to introduce new management information systems. The business was at a point where it had achieved growth and had reached a plateau where consolidation and control were required. The son' style was actually more appropriate to the stage the company was at.

I interviewed the mother and sisters. The mother worked in the caring profession and was on various committees in the local community. The son was more like his mother. The staff liked him because he cared; a trait he inherited from his mother perhaps. The sisters did not work in the business, in fact did not work at all, but both had graduated from a top university with good degrees. They both received a very generous allowance from the company and did attend board meetings. The son had not received any further education but at the request of his father had gone straight into the family business at the age of 16. There was latent resentment that he did not have the opportunity to take a degree and had to work in the business whilst his sisters were paid for not working.

He had everything that was needed to manage the business. Like the straw man in the Wizard of Oz who went to see the wizard to ask for a brain and was told that he did have a brain, what he did not have was a diploma. So it was with the son. He was put on a top management course at a leading business school where he excelled. A new department was set up to develop new opportunities which the father ran and the son became the new business leader. The company introduced new management information systems, including better costing and control and profits improved. The father and son eventually went out for a beer together, and the father accepted that the son was a worthy successor and spent less hours in the business.

12.3. Developing the family successor

So, you are a member of the family and have decided to take a lead role in the business. Do you follow in your predecessors footsteps or do you make a fresh imprint? This may be out of your control in the sense that your predecessor, who may be a parent or sibling, expects you to continue in a prescribed pattern, perhaps, and often more than likely, in their own style. Alternatively, you may be given the opportunity to make a fresh start and begin to mould the business in your own way, putting in practices and procedures that you believe in and, furthermore, feel will benefit or even transform the business. But how do you convince your parents, predecessor or owners to give you that chance? Equally, if you are handing over control how do you ensure that it will be in the best interests of the enterprise?

If the successor is coming from within the family there are two things to consider:

- Is she or he going to be the right person to lead the business?
- Will they want to do it?

A lot will depend upon the aspirations and dreams of the founders or existing business leaders as well as the nature of the business. There is no set formula. For example, some businesses, which may be linked to a current fashion or technology, have a limited life span and may not be suitable for succession. Other family members may have strong views as to the way the company should be run. When considering whether a family member should succeed into the business, there are many things to consider and it is worth spending time considering the full implications and assessing whether it is likely to be the right decision.

There is one thing that is for certain and it is that the transfer of management to a family successor is not necessarily going to be straightforward and is likely to lead to differences of opinion which are often based on emotion rather than rationality. The debates and discussions can sometimes be heated and in quite a number of cases, in my experience, lead to rifts in the family and disturbances and disruption in the business. So how do we ensure that succession of a family is going to work for both the successor and the business?

It is not difficult. It just requires planning. Planning, in my view, is about the most important business activity and is addressed in more detail elsewhere in this book. A good succession plan for a family member taking over the management of the business or one of its functions is as follows.

12.4. Grooming

From an early age it is worth sounding out the potential and possible interest of children. If they feel it is part of their inheritance, they may give the prospect some consideration. Coming into the business to do some part time work after school and weekends will not only give them the opportunity to explore the business but also, potentially give them good commercial experience for whatever careers they might pursue in the future. There is, naturally, the danger that we assume that as children of the owners they should automatically and without question come into the business. Perhaps that is one of the motivations of creating a business. Many family business owners starting out often say to me that they are creating something to secure the future for their children and they anticipate them taking over at some point. As they get older that view can often change and the founders don't want to or can't let go.

In my experience, children of the owners of a family business are usually quite interested in getting involved in the company. After all, they are likely to be living with it at home most of the time, seeing their parents continually discussing the family business on its impact upon the family. It would have been a big part of their life. So why would they not be interested in potentially getting involved in it as a long-term career prospect?

Quite often, I find that children of the owners of a family business are quite proud of the fact and look forward to being involved in it in some way shape or form. Some see it as a simple and easy career option, that their future has already been outlined for them and there is no need to worry about it. On the other hand, there are those children you want to plough their own furrow and have little interest in the family business. This may be because of the nature of the business is not where they see their future. There are also cases where children have embarked upon a career of their own only to find at some point in their life that they are either attracted to the family business or that there is a crisis in the family business and they need to become involved.

Grooming children to come into the family business involves them not only visiting the company or spending some part time working there but gaining an understanding of the values and objectives of the business and what their potential role might be.

12.5. The personality of the successor

What if the personality of the family successor is totally different to that of the founder or the predecessor? There is no guarantee that it will be like mother like daughter or father like son. Furthermore, it could be that the family successor is not a child of the outgoing business leader but a relative such as a nephew, niece or younger brother or sister. The successor may be an adopted child of the parents. Accordingly, we can almost guarantee that their management style is likely to be different. All too often we expect family successors to follow the same path as their predecessors. Sometimes this does happen, but it is not necessarily a good thing. It could be that the business is in a different place in its development. Businesses go through different stages and circumstances in their life and we must consider this when looking at succession. In the early stages of growth greater entrepreneurial skills are required. As the company gets bigger it needs control and consolidation and at times or crisis or poor trading it might need turnaround skills.

12.6. Appropriate further education

There is a view that taking and obtaining a degree in any subject is good enough, regardless of the career opportunities, on the basis that the discipline of taking the degree or any other further education qualification demonstrates commitment and the ability to work. Whilst that is certainly true there must be some value in taking a further education course that is relevant to future career opportunities. If it is a technical, scientific, or engineering enterprise then it is particularly important. Otherwise, a further education qualification in business studies or accounting is very useful. Taking a degree course in Media or Geography is not helpful if the family successor is going into an IT business. We cannot always expect our children to follow in our footsteps, but sometimes they want to, if those footsteps lead to a place where they want to be or if it helps support the lifestyle they aspire to. We need to encourage rather than persuade children to come into the business on the merit that it really is a good career option. Nor should we assume that they ought to be in the business because they are family. If it is a good business and interesting then there is no reason why family members would not want to join in. If we were excited and passionate about it why can't they feel the same way?

Whilst it is not absolutely essential that the family successor takes qualifications that closely match the needs of the business, such as a degree in computing for an IT business or a degree in chemistry for a pharmaceutical enterprise it obviously is advantageous where the business is of a technical nature. However, more crucial is further education related to business management and finance. Both can be accomplished by, for example, the successor qualifying in a technical subject through higher education followed by an MBA or business studies course. In addition, many further education institutes and schools of management offer courses in business management and leadership as well as more focused areas such as marketing and finance. A good grounding in finance is essential for anyone aspiring to lead a business and there are plenty of courses available in financial management for non-financial managers in whichever country you are situated.

12.7. Post education development

It is possible that some of the education in terms of management courses can be taken whilst the family successor is employed in the business and this should be part of the personal development plan. The most important aspect of this plan is not to rush it. Having said that there are situations where a son or daughter has come into the business, possibly too soon because of a personal crisis such as severe ill health, death, divorce etc. In these situations, whilst it may seem the right and honourable things for a child of the predecessor to take on the mantle of running the business, if not managed carefully it could make things worse not better. If these situations arise then it is worth ensuring that there is a mentor for the family successor from within the firm or from outside.

12.8. Integrating into the business.

This should include spending time working in key departments in a real role, not just observing. To be realistic it is not feasible for the family successor to work in every department. Some may be quite small and could not justify another member of staff albeit temporary. In these departments the family successor would observe. To start the whole process it is a good idea to ask the family successor to carry out an initial review of every department and the business in general and to compile a report on their findings. This will be a summary of their understanding of the various functions along with any comments on shortfalls and recommended improvements. They may be inexperienced and naive in business matters but this will be a good way for them to learn about the processes and organisation of the business. We always learn much better by writing things down rather than just taking mental notes. It will also be a test of their analytical skills as these are key in running a successful business. Good business managers know how to analyse.

When I was in my early twenties, I became a management trainee at a company called Ward & Goldstone Limited which was a very large manufacturer of electrical products for both domestic markets and the automotive industry, with several sites across the north west of England. It closed some years ago I believe. Part of our induction was to spend time in several departments. We were tasked with keeping a logbook and had to record our understanding of the business processes, the technical aspects of the department and make comments on where we thought improvements could be made. I filled in the recommendations part of my report with gusto only to be told that a lot it was far too expensive to implement, had been thought of before and didn't work or was just not right. A small percentage of my recommendations however did carry some merit. But the main purpose of the exercise was not to see whether I could come up with recommendations that would work but to see whether I had gained an understanding of the function of the department and whether I could go through the through the mental process of generating intelligent ideas for improvement based on a sensible analysis and understanding of the business.

So, tasking the family successor with both keeping a log and recording their observations about each department is good personal development and encourages them to be observant and to make a real effort to understand the workings of the various functions within the business. Another way of deriving value out of this for both the business and the family successor is to task them with compiling process charts of each department, even if these already exist in the form of procedures manuals. It is good practice as writing down the processes is a better way of learning than simply listening to descriptions of departmental functions by a member of staff. Also, the business may gain some real value by a fresh pair of eyes looking at the way things are done.

Having reviewed processes and procedures the successor should then be requested to comment on them and come up with some recommendations as to where improvements can be made and how. This will not only help them gain experience but also be of potential value to the business, for, after all, if they are going to run the show one would expect them to be making a difference, or at least improving what has gone before. In most cases where this approach has been taken, I have seen recommendations that have been of real value to the business.

Giving them such a project also creates credibility with the management team as well as the staff they are to work with. It is also the best way of learning.

12.9. Letting go

It is important for successors to recognise that 'letting go' is not always easy, especially when you have built the business yourself. It's a bit like letting your son or daughter take the steering wheel for the first time after passing their driving test. You worry that they might take the bend too fast or may not have seen that car about to come out of a junction. Even worse, is when you let them drive on their own for the first time with no one else in the car. You worry as a parent. The business is no different. It has been your vehicle; the one that has carried you thus far and now you have to trust it to someone else's control. Perhaps you created and built it from nothing, or it may have been handed down to you. Letting go is not easy.

In my experience there are two ways of 'letting go': immediately or gradually, and both can be fraught with problems. Letting go immediately sometimes has to happen due to illness or some other sudden event within the family. Letting go immediately can work successfully for the business if:

 a) There has been some preparatory work and the successor is considered competent and qualified enough for the role.
 b) The successor has the confidence and support of the family.
 c) A suitable reporting structure has been set up to keep the family informed.
 d) There is some form of mentoring or support.
 e) The person letting go takes on another role within the business that does not involve them in situations that might lead to conflict with the successor.

Letting go slowly can be a painful process for both parties but it can work providing that is done in a structured way. For example, the person letting go agrees to hand over certain areas of management on a phased basis or takes on a non-executive role such as chair or even acts as adviser. At the end of the day, a lot will depend upon the strength of the personal relationship between the two parties.

Equally the predecessor must also understand that it is often difficult to manage effectively when you are aware that someone is looking over your shoulder. There comes a point that, assuming everything previously described regarding the introduction and development of the successor has been accomplished successfully, we must allow control to pass over. By implementing a programme of regular reviews of performance through one-to-one meetings and board meetings we should gain confidence that succession has worked.

13. Leadership

In my personal experience working with a variety of enterprises in different industrial, commercial, and professional sectors, both family and non-family owned, I have seen two main streams or types of business managers. In terms of management, I believe there are administrators and there are leaders. In my book 'Business Turnaround – How to do it' I discuss the different styles of management, or management types, in more detail and of course there are those who are not really equipped to be managers at all, but surprisingly are able to survive in that role either through influence or apathy.

Administrators are managers who are very good at maintaining status quo and complying with all that is necessary to run the business efficiently and smoothly and they normally do it very well. They manage people efficiently and respectfully and always ensure that the organisation is effective and productive. There are many businesses out there that are successful and profitable and will continue to grow and achieve their objectives run by people that basically administrate.

Business leaders are different. Leaders, in my view, tend to be entrepreneurial and are the ones that will make changes or want to grow and when faced with a difficult situation will treat it as a challenge and work to find a way forward. They will be creative and bold and prepared to take risks. Good leaders are inspirational and motivational. They will thrive on respect and seeing the fruits of their leadership which will be their greatest reward. Yet, many are often modest about their accomplishments and the respect they may have amongst staff. Some are less modest and in the extreme can border on being dictatorial, driving through initiatives through sheer strength of character and persuasive skills. Strong leaders usually find it difficult to accept leadership from others but are likely to accept support through a mentoring role.

13.1. What makes successful leaders?

I believe there are two initial and basic qualities to make a good leader. There are many more of course, but to me the two essential ones to start with are confidence and a decision-making capability. When I was a young man, I always wanted to be a manager. That was my dream, and I worked in a large American owned international company that had operations in Europe and in the UK. I remember going to one of my bosses to ask him about the potential for becoming a manager in the organisation. I asked him what qualification or what qualities I needed to be a manager. He said 'Harry, there is just one quality you need and it's confidence'. He clearly meant personal confidence in myself. That I should believe in myself and not be afraid of others. He was right but it's more than that. It is more than being a confident person. It is confidence in your ability. It's confidence in your plans, your ideas, your thoughts and the way you do things. It is confidence in your relationship with your peers and the people that work for you. If you are confident in yourself and your plans you build confidence in your team. However, there is a big difference between confidence and arrogance.

I was running a manufacturing company of 200 people that was in severe trouble. I was leading the turnaround of the business in an executive capacity. Every day people would come to me and say 'Are we really going to get ourselves out of the situation we are in? Is it going to work out all right?'

Of course, there are only three answers to that question: 'No', 'I don't know', or 'Yes'. I could not very well say 'No' because this questions why I'm there in the first place. To say 'I don't know' is not very conducive to good decisive leadership and is certainly not what people expect so they go away thinking he doesn't know whether we're going to succeed or not. The correct answer is going to be 'Yes', but a qualified 'Yes'. It will be 'yes we will succeed providing that certain objectives are met; certain tasks are carried out and I have your support and contribution in achieving the objectives we have set out'. And of course the final caveat is that nothing can be guaranteed.

One of the most difficult and challenging ingredients required in a good leader is that of making decisions. It is the one thing that people expect from their line manager and certainly from the person at the top. Indecisiveness invokes a loss of confidence by employees in their leader. When I was at the same company, members of staff regularly came to me for decisions regarding what I considered to be minor day to day operational matters. Now, I am not a lover of detail so was reticent about having to spend my time resolving detail minor issues which could have been dealt with locally. The reason I was being asked to make these decisions was because the style of previous management had been 'management by fear' so people were frightened of making decisions themselves to avoid getting blamed if it was the wrong one.

'Management by fear' is a style adopted by many managers in my experience. It means that we will blame you or chastise you when things go wrong, so on that basis make sure you do your work correctly. It is a system of discouragement rather than encouragement. The company had previously been micro-managed, which meant that all the decision making would go to the top and the business manager wanted to be involved in all matters. All that happens when we micro-manage is that staff delegate everything back to us. We cease to lead. We simply manage and administrate.

When I was a middle manager at a large rubber and engineering manufacturing company in England, I had a boss who, if anything went wrong would always ask 'who is to blame'. He wanted to see that person reprimanded when the question should have been 'why' instead of 'who'. It did work. Less mistakes were made, but only because people took fewer risks by using less initiative.

However, making decisions is not just the ability to give an instant yes or no, and probably the worst thing to say is 'leave it with me'. We need to make sure the process of arriving at a decision has at the very least been started. When I worked at KPMG as a management consultant I remember engaging with a client in Birmingham and I had some issues with a complex project I was carrying out. I wanted to make the right decision regarding the approach we should recommend to the client but was uncertain. I needed someone to talk to; to help me make that decision.

I asked to meet up with the partner who headed up my team. He was a person of considerable experience in the management consulting industry and was well respected for intelligence and balanced approach to complex problems. He was also a rugby union referee at the weekends and I wonder whether that gave him the ability to assess situations quickly. I gave him the options before me and said that I needed to decide. What he did was to facilitate a discussion which involved me re-visiting my notes and assessing the various pros and cons of each option. He asked me fundamental questions regarding the impact and implications of the options and how they might meet the objectives of the project. By the end of the discussion I realised that a decision was being made and that I was being guided rather told. It was a decision arrived at through consultation. That is what good managers do. They decide by going through a consultation process. They don't simply say 'leave it with me'.

13.2. Consultation

Consultation is key to good business leadership. Good generals discuss tactics through consultation with their officers before going into battle. So, we should talk to our team and seek their views before deciding. This way they are more likely to be on board with whatever decision is made. We should talk to our peers and even business colleagues or associates outside the business. Then, of course there are business advisers or management consultants.

Many business leaders are reluctant to seek advice from outside on operational or strategic matters, although, naturally, used to going for advice on legal matters or compliance related subjects such as Health and Safety and HR. What often I find is that business leaders are afraid of taking advice externally and reticent about using management consultants because they feel that as the leader they should have all the answers and to go outside means that they are failing.

Of course this is nonsense. Good managers take advice and use external advisers and consultants to supplement their team. Advisers work for you and are there to help not run the business unless you are using them in an interim role. Using advisers and consultants is not a sign of management weakness. It is a sign of strength.

13.3. Empowerment

This is a word is banded around quite a lot but what does it mean? It is more than actually just saying to people 'okay you are empowered! You can now go away and do things yourself.' It is that but it is also much more. To empower people we have to give them the support they need to be empowered. This includes training, resources, tools for the job, access to information etc. It also means support from management in terms of mentoring and counselling and the knowledge that if you do get it wrong you are not going to face a firing squad at dawn.

Empowerment is about creating a culture whereby staff are not afraid of coming to the boss and saying – 'I made a mistake' or 'I got it wrong. It did not go the way I expected or planned.' They are not afraid of making that step into the boss's office. We then need to understand why they got it wrong, not to find blame but to see if measures can be implemented so that it won't happen again. This might mean changing procedures and processes, implementing checks and balances or even accepting that as humans we are all frail and will occasionally forget or make the wrong judgement call. In our processes we need to ensure that the risks of mistakes are minimised.

Otherwise, all that happens is that mistakes are covered up until they are exposed and all hell breaks loose and we have a quest to find someone to blame. So empowerment is also about openness and sharing.

Having said all this, there will be times when mistakes are made through carelessness or even laziness and sometimes plain incompetence. These mistakes are very rarely confessed to of course and in these situations disciplinary measures have to be implemented. However, if we can create a positive culture where there is shared responsibility and people take ownership of their decision making, you will find that mistakes will reduce.

The success of a recent turnaround project I managed as interim CEO of Romag Ltd was partly accomplished through the empowerment of staff. This was actually implemented in practical terms by my HR Manager. She was a young woman, passionate about HR and its role in business. She saw it, as I do, as being more about the development of people rather than maintenance of employment records. Too often it is seen a necessary evil adding no value to the business. In reality good HR management can be one of th key drivers in a business. There were 160 employees and we ensured that every single one of them had some form of training appropriate to their particular role in the business as well as awareness training about business management, finance, marketing etc. We wanted them to take ownership and to believe that this was their business. After all they were stakeholders. Without them there would not be a business.

Everyone in the company was given a personal development plan and everybody was encouraged and allowed to make decisions on their own initiative. They were also encouraged to come up with ideas to improve business performance. Although this was financially incentivised, we found that staff were more grateful of recognition than reward.

So, empowerment is about giving people the tools to be empowered but also giving them recognition and credit. I think it is worth understanding that as a leader you cannot know everything. You cannot possibly know all the details of every function. If you do, then you are micromanaging the business and not leading.

As the business leader your role is strategic. You cannot do every job in your particular business. There are other people that can do it better. It is good to be modest and consult with them, recognise and acknowledge their ideas and, most importantly, give them credit where it is due. That is easily said, but all too often what I see in many businesses is that leaders will not always give credit for good ideas or initiatives instigated by others, particularly subordinates. It is a form of jealousy, the 'why did I not think of this' syndrome.

Many managers might also find it threatening that someone else is coming up with good ideas and that they might be challenged by their superiors as to why they had not thought of it.

I recall one example where a managing director would actually take all the ideas submitted to him by his staff, either formally or informally and then convert them into his own. This included solutions that had been implemented by others. To me this was a sign of insecurity. This person was frightened of other people shining which might he thought might put him in a bad light. After all, he was the boss! He should know everything! He would present these ideas and solutions at board meetings and erase any reports from other members of staff that did not complement his. Of course, all that happened was that staff stopped creating any further ideas because they did not get the credit for it.

This did not benefit the company at all. Giving credit to people and acknowledging and using their ideas in their name is good management. In the end you get the credit because you are managing the business better. Creating a culture where staff feel that they can make a real contribution that will improve business performance or the working environment is professional management and is the way to inspire our staff. It is all part of being a good leader and it is one of the ways to gain the respect of your team members. So, giving credit where its due is really important. Being modest about your role encourages others to contribute and communicate.

I worked with a company where there was one department which seemed to run better than others and where the staff seemed to be happier going about their respective jobs. There was also a good team spirit. When I looked more closely, I found that there was a supervisor who entirely of his own initiative had created a scheme which he called 'the department employee of the month'. Of course, the concept is not new. He had heard that many companies do this many companies so he thought it was a good idea and might help build his own team. He created it by himself in quite an amateurish way. He made up his own paperwork and certificates. It worked extremely well because people got praised and were proud to be told they were employee of the month in that department. It also helped to introduce some competitiveness into the team.

Now, normal procedure, should have been for him to discuss this with his superiors, but he told me he was afraid that he would not get the backing for it. There were two ways of dealing with this. One way was to reprimand him for implementing something which could have implications elsewhere: other employees in other departments might resent it or want something similar. The other option was to turn it into something more positive. What I did was to tell him I thought it was a great initiative, but it would have been great if we could have talked about it first. The reason being that, because it was a such good idea, I wanted to extend it to the whole company and I would like him to manage the scheme. He was delighted and we ran it out with great success, but with the support of the HR and marketing staff. I also told HR to put £100 in his next pay packet as a one-off gift. These small gestures inspired and motivated him even further because he knew that his initiative and been recognised as his. The small financial reward meant a lot. The recognition meant even more.

So, in summary, leading from the front is not about having all the answers. It's about getting the best out of people. It's about inspiring them by giving them direction and by encouraging them to submit their ideas in the full knowledge that they will be listened to and be involved in the decision-making process. It is more about coordination than control.

13.4. Creativity

Someone once said to me that there is a process for everything we do in business. I guess, in the main this is true. However, there are times when we need to be creative and think differently. There is no process for being creative. There is not a textbook that has the formula of creativity. It is driven from within. Artists don't have a process or work to a textbook. If they did we all could be artists. Creativity means challenging the very basis of what we are doing in our business. Creativity is the ability to think about a task or a problem in a new or different way or using our imagination to generate new ideas that can lead to solutions. Being creative enables us to solve complex problems and issues and problems or find better ways of doing things.

If you are creative, you find patterns and make connections to find solutions. Of course, you cannot just suddenly switch to being creative, viz, 'I think I'll go into creative mode for an hour!' We have to think about alternative ways of doing things that may not be conventional or accustomed practice. It means trying to look at things in a more objective way and continually asking ourselves if there are different ways of tacking a particular issue, project or problem. To be creative we have to stop looking at things in a linear fashion such as taking what has been done before and improving it. We have to come at it from a different perspective. As one creative sales director once said to me 'we need to think off the wall!'. To be creative means that we have to be in an environment that stimulates creativity. We cannot be creative sitting in the office looking at the same set of data on the computer screen.

A few years ago I was acting as interim managing director of a very old company involved in the design and manufacture of nursery products. It was a challenging time in the marketplace with customers looking for more innovation. One of the problems we had was that there was nothing fresh coming out of design team. They were in their office everyday doing the same thing and thinking in a linear fashion. They were under pressure to come up with something new. We knew what the customers wanted but it was a question as to how we present that in our new products.

I could see that sitting in the design office working under pressure was not helping. I suggested that they take a few days out; go to London and do nothing but visit the art galleries, fashion houses, department stores etc. They should take time out to see some creativity and beauty, which may have nothing whatsoever to do with what we manufactured or the market we were in. We all get some of our best ideas when we're walking in the park or in the countryside or just doing something that has nothing to do with the business at all. Some other directors thought I was crazy; 'you're giving these guys a holiday!'

They worked in a creative, environment and had to be looked upon as such and that meant being different in terms of how we developed their capability and personal skills. They went away for three days and came back refreshed. They thought differently and were different. Being away from an environment that was constraining allowed them to think more radically and unhindered by the fog of convention. Output from the department became fresher and more alive and sometimes challenging, but it worked.

So, we cannot just be creative by the flick of a switch. We need to be stimulated, the brain needs to be prime pumped and we need fuel in the creative engine.

About was seven to eight years ago I would take a small group business leaders and managers from different organisations on what I called a 'walk and talk workshops'. These used to take place in the wildness of the Yorkshire Dales in England and sometimes the Black Forest or Eifel district in Germany. Talking with other business leaders whilst walking through the countryside where we think about our business in a relaxed environment inspired by the landscape that surrounds us, enabled us to think more rationally and in a more relaxed environment. The conversation would be casual and relaxed with no dominant agenda but an underlying theme of exploration into new and better ways of doing business. So, to think differently it can sometimes help if you are in different environment with different people.

13.5 Leading through uncertain times

Most companies face times of uncertainty in their life. This may be uncertainty about the market or future sales. It could be that we're keeping our head above the water we are not certain as to how sustainable the future is for our business. We're managing to survive but life is tough. Trading is difficult and cash reserves may be being used up. We're wondering when things will things improve. Eventually cash becomes even more critical, but we still manage to keep our head just above the water until we eventually will run out of time and reach the point of no return when we submerge.

When we are planning for the future of our business, we make certain assumptions. For example, most companies that I work with plan with a reasonable degree of certainty that the plan can be achieved. Sometimes they will add in sensitivities regarding sales and cost etc. We can make contingency plans for some events such as fires, server or systems failure and through our risk management policies. We could also be affected by things totally out of our control like a major disaster or economic collapse. It could be international, or it be something regional or local or an event that has only affected your business sector. We cannot possibly plan for such events. You cannot plan for uncertainty. But we can prepare for uncertain times. The way we do this is by making sure we have the capability to respond in terms of resources and skills, and that includes leadership that can deal with a crisis. This is where the difference between and leader is put to the test. If we have a good mix of skills within our business and strong leadership backed up by good financial resources and capacity, we should be able to respond to most situations of uncertainty.

The trick is not to have a plan but to have the resource, the skills, the management and the ability to actually fight our way out of another pleasant uncertain situation.

Real leadership is assumed not given. Leaders are different to managers and managers do not always have to be leaders. A good manager may be someone who can organise, administrate and generally take care of things. They are likely to have reasonable and often good people skills and are quite often technically very capable. A good administrative manager is competent in delivering corporate objectives but not necessarily good at conceiving them. Leaders need to be strategic and inspirational. They also need to be consultative, getting the best from their team through counseling their advice before arriving at a decision. Above they are the ultimate decision makers and implementers. But good leaders do not work in isolation. They get the best from their peers, colleagues, advisers, mentors.

13.6. Mentoring in the leadership role

Mentoring can be of great value and make a difference when we are introducing a successor into a leadership role in the business. A business mentor can take an objective approach when the succeeding leader may have their mind clouded by historical practices and the management style of their predecessors. In addition, they may feel some obligation or pressure to walk in the same footsteps as the predecessor. They may resent this, balk against it or simply ignore it. Mentoring can also be useful to existing leaders and members of the senior management team, and, indeed, is just as appropriate in non-family firms. It could be an ongoing relationship or it could be something short term that is particularly beneficial during times of change.

Regarding a family successor taking over the role of leader of the business, or even a senior position in the organisation, there is great value in them having someone outside the organisation to talk to and act as a sounding board. The desire for a mentor could come from either the new leader or the parents/founders. This can be very helpful where there is:

- a) Some sensitivity with the relationship between the successor and, say, the parents or founders of the business who might expect the new leader to do things their way.
- b) Concern on the part of the founders or parents as to whether their family member, be it child or other relative, is actually up for the role without support.
- c) The desire of the successor to have someone outside of the family to support them.

Otherwise, it could simply be company policy to mentor members of management and staff as part of the company's HR strategy.

The mentor can also act as an intermediary where there are disputes about management style.

One of the biggest issues is that of the predecessor not letting go, despite having the best intentions. Or they may take a back seat from running the business yet still want to comment on the way it is managed, the 'that's not the way I would have done it' syndrome. A good mentor can work between the two parties to resolve these matters whilst accepting the roles of both parties. It is important for successors to recognise that 'letting go' is not always easy, especially when you have built the business yourself.

14. Exiting the family business.

What if there is no successor?

There may be a point where a successor cannot be found or agreed upon. This may simply mean there is no natural succession within the family. It could be that family members have no interest in working in the business as they feel their careers lie elsewhere. This is quite common where, for example, the company has been created due to the founder's redundancy from a specialist sector in say, an engineering or a technology sector. It may have been started to maintain a lifestyle and nothing more and has done its job in that respect. Now the founders are looking to retire and would like to yield some value of the business.

We need to identify succession in the business as early as possible. It is never too early to have a succession plan. If we are certain that there is no successor forthcoming from the family and that an exit is likely to facilitate retirement of the owners then we need to prepare the business for that eventuality.

One of the difficulties one sometimes finds in selling a family business or owner managed business is that its success and continuity is dependent upon one or more individuals, usually the owner or owners. Without these there is no business. It means that anyone buying it would have to bring in their own management team or recruit one. In some cases this is highly probable as the potential buyer may have the resource and feels it can merge two businesses together and save on management overhead. What is important in this scenario is for the owners to ensure that there is a strong middle management team, structure or individuals who can run the business operationally on a day to day basis.

14.1. Management Buy Out

One of the options that might be open to the owners is to consider a Management Buy Out ('MBO') from the existing management team or a member of the team. In my experience it is not always easy to find a management team from existing staff that want to take on the risk of owning and directing a business. Most people are content to be employees rather than employers. They join family companies because they like to work for in the culture of a family business environment. They are often overshadowed by the personalities and driving force of the family.

Again, if an MBO is being considered then it is worthwhile, early on, identifying or recruiting the appropriate personnel who might take on a future leadership role. It may be that there are one or more individuals who could be up for the role and have the necessary potential. It could be that their skills need supplementing by someone outside of the business and it so it may be a combination of a buy out and buy in ('BIMBO').

There will two important requirements in facilitating an MBO:

1) Grooming the future leader or team in preparation for taking over the reins.
2) Access to finance to facilitate the MBO.

14.1.1 *Grooming the future leader/team.*

In the same way that we would groom a family successor we must agree as early as possible who the potential leaders of the MBO will be. This may be done through a series of confidential discussions with individuals who the current business leaders believe have the potential to take on the role. Depending upon their current role and status they should be phased into the role of CEO or other such role. In my experience 12 months up to a maximum of 2 years should be sufficient. This assumes they are already in a senior management position.

A good way of phasing them in is to appoint them as deputy CEO/MD at the appropriate point. This helps also with gaining staff acceptance. It is worth taking into account how popular your choice might be. An unpopular leader can cause real damage. Although it is not a beauty parade, you do want someone who is respected and can lead.

14.1.2 *Accessing finance for the MBO.*

The new team will have to access finance to make the deal – assuming you want some value out of the transaction of course. There are private equity firms, private investors and other lenders that could be interested. The best approach is to engage a corporate finance or management consultancy firm that specialises in raising finance for acquisitions. It is likely that the potential funders will expect the members of the MBO team to put their hand in their pockets as well. This may not be a large amount and is referred to as sweat money – it means that the MBO team is serious and believes in the business so much that members are prepared to take on an element of risk.

Although, as the family owner, it is not your responsibility to raise the finance it will be necessary for you to allow the MBO team sufficient time to do it.

14.2. Selling to a third party.

Selling a company is not always easy. Sometimes it can be straight forward if the company is in a particular niche or sector were there is growth on there are acquirers out there looking to build their portfolio. Of course there are business brokers who will put the company on their books and endeavour to sell it on your behalf. This can be a very expensive route to take as many of them will take a monthly fee and will overvalue the business. Even if the company is not sold they will have made some revenue out of acting on your behalf. An arrangement might be exclusive which gives you no opportunity to pursue other options.

My recommendation if a business sale is considered to be the exit option is to take the appropriate advice from a corporate finance specialist or other qualified advisor. This may be through the accountancy firm that acts as your financial advisor or could be from a management consultancy practice.

The other factor to consider when selling the business is the valuation. As I said previously many brokers will overvalue the business in order to secure the contract to act on your behalf. There are many means and methods and formulae for valuing a business but at the end of the day the real value is only whatever someone wants to pay for it.

If we want to maximise the value of our business for a potential sale then we must plan and prepare for this well in advance. Of course, the best time to sell the business is when it is performing very well with good profitability, cash flow and a healthy balance sheet. However, this may not fit in with the owner's retirement plan as it would be too early. Any future buyer is probably also looking for growth unless they simply want you take your company out of the marketplace and acquire your customers. So, the right time to sell is when the company is profitable but shows further growth potential. If a sale of the business at this point does not fit in with the owners personal plans then we may have to consider a compromise which could include either early retirement or retention in the business until retirement. It is worth remembering that people buy businesses based on historical performance not on what might happen in the future.

Selling the company and staying in the business in some role possibly even as managing director or general manager is another option that is worth considering and could be attractive to potential buyers even if it is only as a short term or interim measure. However, this needs to be thought about carefully. This is no longer your company and you have to come to terms with things being done differently and sometimes in a way that you would not approve.

There is also your relationship with your staff to consider, people who you used to employ and who perhaps reported you to you directly. If you are staying in the business therefore it is important to understand in advance how the acquirer might want the business in the future to be managed. This may not be a problem in the, having seen the success in the past, they may wish to continue with the same management style.

Another option to consider is the potential merger with another family business in a similar or the same sector. It could be a competitor. You may know someone well enough to approach them yourself.

Exiting your family business can become an emotional rollercoaster. However, it may be the opportunity to raise some value out of the business would you have built successfully, to get something back for the blood, sweat and tears you have poured into the enterprise. You have created a business, employed people, served a business community and created something of value. It is something to look back on with pride. This is why it is important to ensure that we spend time considering who we might want to sell the business to and how we can ensure its continuity.

www.ingramcontent.com/pod-product-compliance
Lightning Source LLC
Chambersburg PA
CBHW060842220526
45466CB00003B/1201